Pentecost 2

Proclamation 4

Aids for Interpreting
the Lessons of the Church Year

Pentecost 2

David M. Greenhaw

Series B

FORTRESS PRESS   MINNEAPOLIS

PROCLAMATION 4
Aids for Interpreting the Lessons of the Church Year
Series B: Pentecost 2

Copyright © 1991 Augsburg Fortress. All rights reserved. Except for brief quotations in critical articles or reviews, no part of this book may be reproduced in any manner without prior written permission from the publisher. Write to: Permissions, Augsburg Fortress, 426 S. Fifth St., Box 1209, Minneapolis, MN 55440.

Scripture quotations unless otherwise noted are from the New Revised Standard Version of the Bible, copyright © 1989 by the Division of Christian Education of the National Council of Churches of Christ in the United States of America.

Library of Congress Cataloging-in-Publication Data

(Revised for ser. B, vols. 5–8)

Proclamation 4.

    Consists of 24 volumes in 3 series designated A, B, and C, which correspond to the cycles of the three year lectionary. Each series contains 8 basic volumes with the following titles: [1] Advent-Christmas, [2] Epiphany, [3] Lent, [4] Holy Week, [5] Easter, [6] Pentecost 1, [7] Pentecost 2, and [8] Pentecost 3. In addition there are four volumes on the lesser festivals.
    By Christopher R. Seitz and others.
    Includes bibliographies.
    1. Bible—Homiletical use. 2. Bible—Liturgical lessons, English. 3. Bible—Criticism, interpretation, etc. 4. Common lectionary. 5. Church year.
I. Seitz, Christopher R. II. Title: Proclamation four.
BS534.5.P765   1991   264'.34   88-10982
ISBN 0-8006-4175-2 (series B, Pentecost 2)

The paper used in this publication meets the minimum requirements of American National Standard for Information Sciences—Permanence of Paper for Printed Library Materials, ANSI Z329.48-1984. ∞™

Manufactured in the U.S.A.   AF 1-4175
95   94   93   92   91   1   2   3   4   5   6   7   8   9   10

Contents

The Tenth Sunday after Pentecost	7
The Eleventh Sunday after Pentecost	13
The Twelfth Sunday after Pentecost	19
The Thirteenth Sunday after Pentecost	25
The Fourteenth Sunday after Pentecost	30
The Fifteenth Sunday after Pentecost	36
The Sixteenth Sunday after Pentecost	40
The Seventeenth Sunday after Pentecost	46
The Eighteenth Sunday after Pentecost	52
The Nineteenth Sunday after Pentecost	58

The Tenth Sunday after Pentecost

Lutheran	Roman Catholic	Episcopal	Common Lectionary
Exod. 24:3-11	2 Kings 4:42-44	2 Kings 2:1-15	2 Sam. 12:1-14
Eph. 4:1-7, 11-16	Eph. 4:1-6	Eph. 4:1-7, 11-16	Eph. 3:14-21
John 6:1-15	John 6:1-15	Mark 6:45-52	John 6:1-15

FIRST LESSON: EXODUS 24:3-11

This text harks back to the narrative from Exodus 19. Between chapters 19 and 24 are the Decalogue and the laws that form the basis of the covenant set in force by Moses' words, "See the blood of the covenant that the LORD has made with you in accordance with all these words" (v. 8).

The passage describes the ritual sequence of sealing the covenant. Moses comes to the people and tells them all the words of the Lord and all the ordinances. The people respond in unison that they will do what the Lord has spoken. Moses writes the words, builds an altar, and sends young men to offer burnt offerings. Moses divides the blood of the offering, throws half of it on the altar and saves the other half for the conclusion of the ritual. Moses reads aloud the covenant into which the people are entering. Again the people respond that they will do what the Lord has spoken. At this juncture, however, the people make an additional affirmation: They will do what the Lord has spoken *and* they will be obedient. Moses concludes the ritual by throwing the remaining blood on the people and proclaiming the covenant in force.

In throwing the blood and pronouncing the words, Moses mediates God's commitment to the covenant. Israel's commitment to the covenant, although signaled in verse 3 by their stated intention to do what the Lord has spoken, is not consummated until they add the phrase "and we will be obedient" (v. 7).

The significance of this commitment to obedience is found in Exodus 19. In verse 19:5, following a brief recital of Yahweh's saving activity on behalf of Israel, Yahweh sets the conditions for the covenant: "Now therefore, if you *obey* my voice and keep my covenant, you shall be my treasured possession out of all the peoples." Obedience is a condition without which there is no basis for the establishment of this covenant. When the people pledge obedience, the covenant is established.

Obedience in both its older English usage and in the Hebrew *shema* (translated as "obedience") is a derivative of the word for *hearing*. To obey is to hear. The English word *heed* may give a fuller sense of what is meant by obedience. To heed the word of another is to take note of it and to respond accordingly. When Israel adds that they will not only do what the Lord has said, but will also obey, they have indicated their commitment to continue to hear/heed what the Lord says. The covenant that is set into force is not a static law that will simply be followed; it is a living relationship between the God who has brought the people out of bondage and the people who now commit themselves to this God.

When Israel commits to obeying/hearing Yahweh, a balance in the covenant is completed. Note well that the offer of covenant initiated in 19:5 follows a recital of Yahweh's liberating activity for Israel's sake. The covenant is founded on the deliverance from Egyptian bondage. The entire exodus event begins with Yahweh hearing (*shema*) the cry of the people because of their taskmasters (Exod. 3:7). Yahweh's history of hearing the people, of heeding their suffering, is balanced in the covenant by Israel's commitment to obey (*shema*) the Lord.

Resistance to obedience is not uncommon in our time. The very word obey can cause the hair to stand up on the back of our necks. So conditioned are we to free thinking and choosing our own way, that a call to obedience smacks of acquiescence to oppression. Such would be the case with Israel's pledge to obedience, if not for the history of God's hearing the cries of the people. They submit themselves to obedience to the one who likewise submits to their suffering. The condition God sets for covenant making, that the people obey God's words, is already conditioned on God's side by a faithfulness in hearing their cries of oppression. Obedience, then, is not relinquishing oneself to a tyrannical will, but submitting your life to this one who hears and frees.

ALTERNATIVE FIRST LESSON: 2 SAMUEL 12:1-14

The story of Nathan confronting David with the death of Uriah is carefully crafted. It begins with "the thing that David had done" (11:27). The Lord sends Nathan to David, and Nathan proceeds by telling David a parable. As the parable unfolds, David's sympathies are drawn in and he champions the side of good over evil. Then in a remarkably climactic moment, Nathan turns the tables and accuses David saying, "You are the man!" Trapped by his own zeal for justice, David confesses his sin.

David, a king with humble beginnings, has become all too familiar with the world of power politics. He, like many today, has come to believe that what really matters is the power of kings and rulers. The lives of ordinary people are insignificant (and in Uriah's case expendable) when compared to the "important" lives of the "important people." The story suggests that things are otherwise. Faithful rulers in Israel must execute justice for all God's people, from the "least" to the "greatest." This is the call to the rulers of Israel; it is a call shared by those who would be faithful rulers today. In the case of David, as told in this story, the call to such faithful ruling has not been heeded and the prophet Nathan comes to judge.

Perhaps one of the most significant aspects of this lection is that Nathan is successful in judging the king. It would be easy enough to imagine it going otherwise. Having heard the prophet out, the king could have thanked the prophet for "the nice message," as so many Sunday morning worshipers do when shaking the pastor's hand as they walk out of church. The king could have gone unmoved by the prophet's words, but he didn't. He was moved by this encounter with the prophet. In our day, it is almost inconceivable that a religious person could have such an impact on a national leader. It is easy enough to imagine a photo opportunity between a denominational leader and the president, but it is quite unlikely that a prophetic word of judgment could be spoken or heard in such an audience.

It is not clear how or why the king granted Nathan an audience; perhaps it was because the prophet in this story wears the garb of a dramatist. After all, Nathan came telling a story, presenting a moving play about a rich man and a poor man. It could be that Shakespeare had something like the encounter between Nathan and David in mind when Hamlet soliloquizes: "The play's the thing wherin I'll catch the conscience of the king." (*Hamlet*, Act II, Scene II). Catching the conscience of the "king," be it David or Claudius, or for that matter Bush or Gorbachev, is not something done head-on. It may require, as in this text, the artful rendering of a prophetic dramatist.

It is not altogether clear who the contemporary prophets are. It may be that among the most influential prophets today are dramatists, playwrights, and filmmakers. In the presentation of their dramas they do indeed have the potential to "catch the conscience." Or it might just be that the dramatic liturgies of the church are not as irrelevant as is sometimes suspected, but are capable of the sort of artful renderings with which Nathan caught the conscience of the king. As the liturgy unfolds, our sympathies are drawn in and we, like David, can become champions for the side of good over evil.

SECOND LESSON: EPHESIANS 4:1-7, 11-16

The lack of a clear reference to a particular setting or circumstance makes Ephesians one of the most difficult New Testament letters to interpret. The problem is not that its language is obscure or its sequence convoluted, but that its style is so general as to apply to almost any situation. It could be that the author is addressing a community that has experienced a noble history of faithfulness and cooperation. Or it could be that the letter is addressed to a community with deep and troubling divisions. The references to specific settings are insufficient to determine much about the audience.

Given the broad possibilities for interpretation, it is important to attend carefully to the overarching theme in the passage, namely the urge for unity. The text makes clear that what is to be sought is unity—oneness in hope, Lord, faith, Spirit, baptism, and God. The parts are to join together into the whole. By attending to the theme of unity the text is readily applicable to any Christian community, ancient or modern.

Unity is explicitly mentioned twice in this lection. In verse 3 the author exhorts to maintain or keep unity. Verse 13 follows the exhortation to build up the body of Christ until unity is attained or met. On the one hand, unity is presumed to already exist and therefore is to be maintained; on the other hand, unity is still something to be attained. There is a tension between maintaining and attaining. Unity is both present and absent.

In the contrast between maintaining and attaining unity the text addresses a crucial issue of Christian life. While confessing oneness in Christ, the church experiences diversity and frequent divisiveness. On so many matters the people of God in Jesus Christ differ, disagree, and divide. Although there is a sense of unity among Christians, there is also a clear sense of radical difference. Perhaps a generation ago it was more possible to believe in a homogeneous world where difference only existed outside the community of the church. Now it is becoming clear that difference and diversity are present within the church as well. The experience of unity, when and if it is experienced, is accompanied by the recognition of division, special interests, and factionalism.

The call of Christians is to the one hope (v. 4) and it is this hope that forms the basis for unity. It is not that the church or Christians are now one, but that they now hold to one hope for finally being one. The unity that exists now, and that is to be maintained, is the unity of a single hope. The content of that single hope is that the future holds the promise of full unity in Christ. Like many roads leading to the same destination, the church is comprised of diverse persons, perspectives, and gifts, all leading to a horizon of oneness.

By beginning with the presumption of unity that is to be maintained, the text then moves to the frank recognition of the divisiveness that exists. It cautions not to be carried away by divisiveness (v. 14), but to hold fast to the promised future of unity.

The Tenth Sunday after Pentecost

In short, the letter exhorts: Be united by the persistent call to unity, even when not yet united. The present experience of unity is found in the experience of its absence *and* in the persistent hope of its coming. The faithful church is not one with a homogeneous present, but one with a future in Christ where the fullness of unity will be met.

GOSPEL: JOHN 6:1-15

This familiar story, like many familiar stories, has several elements that are easily overlooked. As the beginning of a larger unit, the narrative places emphasis on themes to be treated later. By attending only to the more obvious elements in the story, especially the feeding of the five thousand, it is possible to miss other subtle, but nonetheless significant, elements.

Chief among the more subtle elements is "seeing." On two occasions what *the crowd* sees is described (vv. 2 and 14) and on two occasions what *Jesus* sees is described (vv. 5 and 15). What the crowd sees frames the pericope. The crowd sees signs. At the beginning, having seen the signs Jesus "did on those who were diseased," the crowd followed him. At the conclusion, having seen the most recent sign he had done, they identify Jesus as the "prophet who is to come into the world." What Jesus sees frames the action in the story. Jesus sees the crowd; he sees them coming to him (v. 5) and perceives they are about to make him king (v. 15).

"Seeing" develops into a major theme in the larger unit, of which this pericope is the beginning. In John 6:26 Jesus accuses the crowd of pursuing him for the wrong reason: "you are looking for me, not because you saw signs, but because you ate your fill of the loaves." In 6:36 Jesus says, "you have seen me and yet do not believe." And in 6:40 he says, "This is indeed the will of my Father, that all who see the Son and believe in him may have eternal life." Although seeing is important, simply seeing is not enough. One is to see and, from what one has seen, believe.

What a person believes is closely related to what is seen. This is what lies behind such sayings as: "I'll believe it when I see it," and "I don't believe my eyes." When we see something that is at variance with what we traditionally believe, we either change our belief or discount what we have seen. The crowd, after having seen the sign Jesus performed, changed their belief about who Jesus was. No longer did they believe him to be an ordinary person, now they believed him to be the "prophet who is to come into the world."

From what the crowd has seen of Jesus they believe he is worth following and that he is the prophet who is to come. But the text gives warrant to think that these beliefs, even though laudable, are not what one is to believe from what has been seen. The crowd does not yet believe fully because they have not yet rightly interpreted what they have seen. Although those who see firsthand are in an advantaged position, it is a lost advantage unless what is seen leads to belief. Those who have not seen firsthand, which surely includes the Johannine community as well as the contemporary congregation, have open to them the possibility of seeing and believing if they will look at the signs described to them. Since seeing plays such an important role in chapter six and since the smaller unit (John 6:1-15) is framed by two allusions to seeing, the reader is given warning to carefully look at what there is to see in the story and to attend to what is to be believed from what is seen.

The action is fairly straightforward: Jesus asks Philip how bread is to be bought for so many; Philip answers that there are insufficient financial resources to feed them; Andrew says there are insufficient foodstuffs to feed them; Jesus takes the insufficient foodstuffs, gives thanks, and distributes them, they eat their fill; Jesus tells the disciples to gather the leftover fragments; they do so and there are twelve baskets of leftover bread.

The text indicates that Jesus foreknows the outcome of the events that transpire. The disciples inaccurately predict the outcome. The disciples operate out of the assumption that there is a scarcity, and given the scarcity it will not be possible to feed the five thousand. By contrast, Jesus operates out of the assumption that there is an abundance. As it becomes clear, there is a sufficient amount of fish and an abundance of bread.

What Jesus sees and believes is that with God there is no scarcity but an abundance. The "sign" that is portrayed in this story attempts to challenge a fundamental belief about scarcity. It is assumed by the disciples that the resources necessary to feed the crowd are scarce. The sign Jesus performs shows just the opposite. In what Jesus shows and in what is to be believed there is no scarcity, but an abundance. It is no accident that two verses of the story are dedicated to making clear that there was an abundance leftover.

This story challenges our foundational belief in scarcity. Our whole society is organized around the belief that what it takes to have life is in short supply. There is a scarcity of time, money, and energy. Such a belief serves a useful function; it is what motivates people to work and consume sufficiently to keep the economy running. By the same token it makes of us driven and acquisitive creatures trying to grab all we can while there is still something to be grabbed. In this story there is not only enough, but there is an abundance. The bread in the story is sufficient not just for life, but for eternal life.

As one of the communities that has open to them the possibility of seeing and believing anew, the contemporary Christian congregation might come to believe that with God there is an abundance of what it takes to live. It all depends on what is seen. If we see only the panicky drive to acquire and consume that so thoroughly infects our common life, we will continue to believe that there is a scarcity. If, however, we see the abundance made manifest in this sign of Jesus, then we may be liberated from our belief in scarcity.

If the crowds are to be fed, which belief will liberate us to share what we have: a belief in scarcity? or a belief in God's abundance?

The Eleventh Sunday after Pentecost

Lutheran	Roman Catholic	Episcopal	Common Lectionary
Exod. 16:2-15	Exod. 16:2-4, 12-15	Exod. 16:2-4, 9-15	2 Sam. 12:15b-24
Eph. 4:17-24	Eph. 4:17, 20-24	Eph. 4:17-25	Eph. 4:1-6
John 6:24-35	John 6:24-35	John 6:24-35	John 6:24-35

FIRST LESSON: EXODUS 16:2-15

A story about bread in the wilderness given from the hands of God, this tale begins with murmuring born of hunger. The ones who murmur are the whole congregation of the people of Israel. To whom they direct their murmurings is a key to interpreting this story.

It is against Moses and Aaron that the people of Israel murmur (v. 2). They are distressed because they are being overtaken with hunger. The fleshpots of Egypt are surely preferable to starvation in the wilderness. Before Moses and Aaron respond to the people's complaint, God responds by promising "bread from heaven" (v. 4). Moses and Aaron, who are clearly intermediaries in this story, pass on to the congregation what they have received from God. But they do more than pass on the promise God gives them; they refuse to accept the murmurings directed toward them. It is not they who should be held accountable for the starvation in the wilderness; it is God. Nor is it they who should be given credit for feeding the starving ones with bread from heaven; again, it is God.

The newly formed congregation of Israel does not yet understand the pattern of relation to this God who has brought them out of slavery in Egypt. The pattern runs like this: the people cry out of their suffering, and God hears and responds (see Exod. 3:7). Israel, not yet accustomed to this pattern, has grown dependent on its leaders—Moses and Aaron. If hunger is overtaking them, they are sure it is Moses and Aaron who are to blame, and Moses and Aaron who must act to remedy the problem. Relying on an unseen God when their stomachs are empty is expecting too much. They want action now, from the ones close at hand.

Although Israel is slow to catch on to the pattern of relation to God, the reader is given little room to miss the point. Four times in five verses the reader is told that God has heard Israel's murmurings (vv. 7, 8, 9, 12). It is because God has heard their murmurings that the bread from heaven is given. The focus on the hearing of God is significant, because until Israel and the hearers of the story understand that God hears their murmurings, they will not understand it is God who gives bread.

The bread discovered at dawn is not just bread, it is bread from heaven, given by God. Giving bread to the hungry ones is central to the character of the God who enters into relationship with this people. Coming to know this God is coming to know that this God hears the cries and murmurs of hungry people and responds by giving bread.

This lesson about God remains important for Israel throughout its history. It is replayed in various ways by prophets and wisdom teachers, even psalmists and faithful kings. It is also a lesson to be replayed by faithful leaders, teachers, and preachers in our own time. It is the very character of God to hear the cries of those who hunger and suffer, and not to rest until they are fed.

ALTERNATIVE FIRST LESSON: 2 SAMUEL 12:15b-24

Nathan pronounced God's judgment on David, that "the child that is born to you shall die" (2 Sam. 12:14), and so in these verses we have the story of the child's dying. The story is important to the narrator of this story only as it relates to David's reaction to the death. The narrator gives neither the child's name nor gender; it is simply "the child."

David suffers the child's dying; he grieves openly and passionately. By stark contrast, he does not grieve the child's death. When word comes that the child is dead, even before it is spoken to him, David rises from his grief and ends his fasting. The narrator does not suggest that David's grief for the dying of the child is feigned. The grief is apparently real, sincere. Nevertheless, it ends abruptly. Although it is not completely clear what the narrator thinks of this abrupt change in David's mood, it is surely the case that the portrayal of the grief's end is abrupt. Tersely the point is made: The child is dead, there is nothing more to do. The point is made clear by David's question: "Can I bring him back again?"

David's grief over his children is a repeated theme in these narratives. The grief over this child is solely related to the act of dying. (Compare this to David's grief over Absalom, 2 Sam. 18:24-33). This child has little personal history and David knows already that there is no future with the child, because Nathan has predicted it. With no history and no future, all that is left is a present in which the child is dying. David grieves the dying in the present; when death comes he coolly moves on.

The lack of a personal history for this child, a point the narrator makes by excluding any reference to name or gender, cannot fully obscure the violent history related to the child's conception. That David is able to grieve the child's dying is testimony to David's compassion. That he is quick to move on is testimony to his hope for a future beyond guilt. Indeed, as the story indicates, there will be other futures (v. 24); Solomon is born. It is important to note that unlike the now dead child, the narrator tells us the name and gender of this child. Solomon is a child with a history and a future and through him the reign of David has a future as well.

SECOND LESSON: EPHESIANS 4:17-25

The portion of this text translated in the Revised Standard Version as "you must no longer live as the Gentiles do" (v. 17), contains the Greek word *peripateō*, which can be translated as "walk." This same word is used repeatedly in Ephesians 4-6. In fact, it is used so often there that it might be appropriate to title those chapters after the old hymn, "A Closer Walk with Thee." According to this text, not all walks are closer walks with God. Some walks are marked by futility, misunderstanding, and alienation; others are marked by righteousness and holiness. There is a proper walk, a proper path to follow, a proper way to proceed, and the readers are urged to walk that walk. On the other hand, there is an improper walk, a misguided path, a wrong way to proceed, and the readers are exhorted not to walk that one.

The difference between the two walks has to do with the truth that is in Jesus (v. 21). The readers are warned that they must not take the wrong way; they must not walk in the way that leads to futility, darkness, and alienation and that ends in licentiousness, greed, and uncleanness. If they have taken this path, walked this walk, then they have not learned what there is to learn in Christ: "That is not the way you learned Christ!" (v. 20).

The clear implication is that learning what there is to learn in Christ, that is, coming to the truth that is in Jesus, involves making a radical change. The author indicates the radicality of this change by starkly painting the "former way" (v. 22). The former way is marked by almost every conceivable bad thing. It is corrupt, unclean, callous, alienated, darkened in understanding and filled with ignorance, deceitful lusts, futility, and hardness of heart. It would be difficult to imagine a more complete catalog of evils from which one is to depart. The "old nature" is so bad the reader can hardly avoid choosing the other way, putting on the "new nature."

Although the old nature is painted thoroughly and starkly in these verses, the new nature is barely sketched. The contrast to the long catalog of evils is only the brief phrase "created according to the likeness of God in true righteousness and holiness" (v. 24). Suggestive as this phrase may be, it is scarcely a counterbalance to the lengthy description on the other side. The emphasis is on what is left behind. The radical change called for is first a change away from something bad.

It is as if one stands at a fork in a road. To walk down one road is to make a dreadful mistake, because it is filled with many evil things. What lies down the other road is not yet completely clear, but it is clearly the preferred road. The one who walks down the latter road will be taking a closer walk with God.

Although the description of the new nature is brief and quite broad, the need for change is clearly conveyed. The Christian life involves a change from one way of life to another. It is not more of the same; it is instead a new way of life and involves a new walk. For contemporary Christians, unable to distinguish being a good Christian from being a good person, the starkness of the change described in this text is instructive. The description of the Christian life in this portion of Ephesians does not list all the things a good Christian does. There is no checklist of rules to follow or tasks to perform. Instead, there is a call to walk in faithfulness to God. Each step of the way will require a new inquiry into what it means to live the Christian life.

GOSPEL: JOHN 6:24-35

This pericope and the one that follows it include an interpretation of Moses and the manna in the wilderness. Although the manna story is only a piece of this text, it provides a focal point for interpreting the whole.

Moses and manna are first referred to by the crowd who has followed Jesus. Apparently this is the same crowd, the five thousand, who had been fed their fill the previous day. They want to know what sign Jesus does that they may believe him. They need a sign because their forebears had a sign—manna in the wilderness. Jesus responds by saying that Moses did not give them bread from heaven, but that it was "my Father" who gave the true bread.

The response Jesus gives is a corrective to the crowd's interpretation of the manna story. Lest the crowd think that Moses did the feeding, Jesus makes it clear that it was God. Whatever role Moses had in the manna story was subservient to what God was doing. This corrective is all the more important in the light of the opening exchange of the current dialogue. Near the beginning of the discourse, Jesus rebukes the crowd for not understanding or heeding the sign that they saw, namely the feeding of the five thousand. He says, "You are looking for me, not because you saw signs, but because you ate your fill of the loaves" (v. 26). The crowd has twice misinterpreted a feeding. In the feeding associated with Moses and now in the one associated with Jesus they have overlooked God's action; they have failed to see it as a sign.

Between the discussion of the two feedings, there is a somewhat disjointed series of exchanges. A bit like the children's game "Barrel of Monkeys," this discourse is fragilely linked together. The game consists of a small barrel-shaped container with about a dozen plastic monkeys with outstretched arms. The game is played by pouring the monkeys onto the floor and then attempting to successively link the monkeys' arms together into a chain and return them to the barrel. The game is made difficult because the monkeys are barely connected when their arms are linked. Like the arms of the monkeys in the children's game, the exchanges in this dialogue between Jesus and the crowd are barely linked together. Only by the narrowest of connections, a repeated reference to work, are the portions of this discussion held together.

In four verses the word "work" is used in some form, five times. The exchange begins (v. 27) when Jesus speaks of food that endures to eternal life as opposed to food that perishes, and admonishes the crowd to work (*ergazomai*) for the food that endures. The crowd does not respond to Jesus' words about enduring food, but instead focus on his mention of work. They want to know what they must do to work the works of God. Work makes the connection to the next exchange also, but Jesus uses it very differently from how the crowd has used it. In verse 27 Jesus uses the word "work" as a means to accomplish something, that is, as labor. When the crowd uses it they are asking about doing God's work. Jesus responds in verse 29 using work in an altogether different way—here it refers to what God has accomplished. One more time, in verse 30, a connection between exchanges is made by referring to work. This time the crowd asks about signs and questions Jesus about what works he might do that they can believe him.

The crowd uses the word "work" to refer to what they must do or what Jesus must do. Jesus uses the word at first to refer to labor and then to refer to what God accomplishes. The crowd understands work as something you do in the moment and for the moment. It passes and must be done again. It is what it is and nothing more. When they speak of work, they are speaking of human work, perhaps done for God, but nonetheless human work. Jesus, however, is speaking of a work of God, something God has done. It is not only what it is, but it is also a sign, an indicator of something more.

As in their understanding of Moses and the manna, and the feeding of the five thousand, the crowd's understanding of work is too mundane. The crowd seeks those things—food, work, and signs—that allow them to bide their time, to get by, to make it to the next meal, the next job, the next miracle. Jesus rebukes them for seeking that which only bides their time and charges them to seek that which will abide, endure, persist. (When Jesus speaks of food that endures, the Greek word is *menō*, which is translated as *endures, remains,* or, elsewhere in the Fourth Gospel, as *abide.*)

The difference between biding one's time and that which abides is what is at the center of the work that God has done in Jesus. In verse 33 Jesus says, "For the bread of God is that which comes down from heaven, and gives life to the world." What God has done is give life to the world. The exact character of that life is not fully spelled out at this point in the Fourth Gospel, but this much is already clear: It is a life worth seeking (v. 26), it is a life that endures to eternal life (v. 27). In Jesus, God is doing an important work that changes all of life, transforms human endeavor, and promises eternal life.

The contemporary congregation shares much in common with the crowd. Many are caught in a variety of endeavors that amount to little more than biding one's time, enduring not to eternal life, but until one dies. And few see signs; things are what they are and nothing more. Without the ability to see signs, to see God at work in the world, one correctly concludes that what one sees is what one gets. If that is the case, then the advertisers are right and the most logical course of action is to "grab all the gusto, while there is still gusto to be grabbed." When signs can be seen, when it is possible to see the agency of God in the actions of a human agent like Moses or Jesus, at the very least there is more to the world than first imagined. If that is the case, then our course of action need not be reduced to the wild acquisitiveness that so much characterizes our culture. Our lives could be open to acts that do more than first is apparent.

The Twelfth Sunday after Pentecost

Lutheran	Roman Catholic	Episcopal	Common Lectionary
1 Kings 19:4-8	1 Kings 19:4-8	Deut. 8:1-10	2 Sam. 18:1, 5, 9-15
Eph. 4:30—5:2	Eph. 4:30—5:2	Eph. 4:30—5:2	Eph. 4:25—5:2
John 6:41-51	John 6:41-51	John 6:37-51	John 6:35, 41-51

FIRST LESSON: 1 KINGS 19:4-8

Elijah has made Queen Jezebel angry and she has put a contract out on his life. He is in deep trouble back home. He is certain to die if he stays home. So, in order to save his life, he flees. After he has successfully escaped with his life, he wants nothing more than to die. The irony of Elijah asking that his life be taken away in the wilderness after fleeing for his life from Jezebel's wrath has been noted by several biblical scholars (for instance, Walter Brueggemann, Richard Nelson). Afraid that he might be killed, Elijah took refuge in the wilderness. Once in the wilderness, however, he no longer had a desire to live, saying: "It is enough; now, O LORD, take away my life" (v. 4). How is it that one whose passion for living was sufficient to escape execution would now rather die than go on living?

Before Elijah fled, he was in his homeland. Troubled as he and his people were, he was at home. When he left home, he went into the wilderness. In the Hebrew Bible, the figure of the wilderness frequently echoes with the ambiguity of leaving behind trouble only to face a desolate future. Recall the movement into the wilderness described in Exodus. To enter the wilderness means leaving behind a troubled past but also looking forward to an uncertain and frightening future. The future Elijah faces in the wilderness is a desolate one. He has fulfilled his prophetic office, but he is now a prophet without a people. He has been vigilant for God, but now he is alone in the wilderness. He has a broken past, no future, and this solitary wilderness for a present—life is no longer worth living and he wishes to die.

Then an angel touches him and commands him to "arise and eat." Placed before him are a cake and water, basic elements for living. Over against the death to which Elijah was resigning himself, the angel presents fundamental elements of life. While the wilderness is a place filled with ambiguity, bread in the wilderness is an unambiguous affirmation of life: "Look here, Elijah, there is food to eat and water to drink, all is not lost."

The concluding verse replays the familiar phrase "forty days and forty nights" (v. 8). Forty days and forty nights indicate a period of transition. Things will not be the way they are forever, but they are this way for a while. When Elijah entered the wilderness, he had a desolate future and a broken past; after the visit from the angel, the desolation of his future has subsided a little, but things are still uncertain. With the gift of bread Elijah lives—death is pushed back for a while. But, as is indicated by the phrase forty days and forty nights, bread and water are transitional. Alone, they will not suffice to keep death away forever. Bread and water give a present to one with a broken past and no hope for a future, but a present is not enough for living. Sooner or later living requires a future. This story of Elijah is not resolved until a future is secured; only then is Elijah's threatened life (see vv. 10 and 14) restored to him.

The gift of bread is a powerful gift. Bread on its own, however, is not enough. Providing food for those with a broken past and a desolate future is a remarkable, even miraculous, event that holds death at bay. But holding death at bay is not the same thing as giving life. Food without a future will finally give no life. Human beings do not live by "bread alone" (Matt. 4:4), but by food and a hopeful future. Congregation's efforts to respond to world hunger and the crisis of homelessness will be fruitful and faithful if they both provide a present and work to secure a future for the hungry ones.

ALTERNATIVE FIRST LESSON: 2 SAMUEL 18:1, 5, 9-15

The lectionary carefully gathers together the threads of the story of the death of Absalom. The son of David who leads a coup d'etat against his father is killed by his father's most trusted general. David had asked that his armies "deal gently for my sake with the young man Absalom" (v. 5). Killed while hanging helplessly from an oak tree, he clearly was not dealt with gently.

The narrator goes to great lengths to make the point that David is not present at the battle. Verses 2-5 deal with the king's decision to leave the battlefield and return to the city. Since the king is not present in battle, he is not present when Absalom dies. The events of the day, however, will not be long hidden from him. It is precisely this point the soldier who sees Absalom hanging from a tree makes when he reports it to Joab. He says, "There is nothing hidden from the king" (v. 13). The saying, although said in passing, is key to interpreting the lection. Indeed, nothing will ultimately be hidden from the king. In fact, the narrator may be suggesting that in some fashion the death of Absalom was not hidden from David even before it happened. Despite David's plea that the armies "deal gently with the young man Absalom," he must have known this was not possible. Even his choice of words reflects his ambiguity about the request. He says "deal gently." He does not strictly forbid killing him. That the armies could deal gently with the leader of the rebellion was not possible. As is clear from the argument David's own soldiers make to him, the leader of the armies is greater than ten thousand soldiers (vv. 3-4). David does not go to the battlefield, he is not present at the killing, but he knows Absalom must die and he cannot hide from the facts for long.

Perhaps more than any other character in the Bible, David is portrayed in the most unflinchingly human terms. Even though he is a heroic figure in these stories, he is an ambiguous hero at best. Perhaps, had he gone into battle himself, he could have ensured that Absalom would have been dealt with gently. But this was not really a possibility. David is both king and father. As king, he *must* oversee the killing of a rebel; as father, he cannot oversee the killing of his son. He would like to hide from the facts, but he cannot, they haunt him, catch up with him, refuse to let him go. The passing remark of the soldier says it all: "There is nothing hidden from the king." Woe to the king! Would that he could hide from the anguish coming his way! Absalom is killed and David's kingdom is preserved. Absalom is killed and another of David's children is lost. Who can count the gain and loss? Who can bear the sacrifice?

There is no neat fit between the circumstances of David's life and our own. There are circumstances in our lives, however, where we too find ourselves unable to hide. There are tragic sequences of events from which we cannot fully escape. Would that it would be otherwise; but it is not! Woe to anyone from whom there is nothing hidden!

SECOND LESSON: EPHESIANS 4:25—5:2

Having set the scene in the preceding verses (vv. 17-24), this portion of Ephesians begins the exploration of what it would be like to walk as a Christian walks. The path that lies ahead for the Christian is described, with directions on how to proceed. It is not a path without difficulties, but it is a path filled with the promise of a faithful and fruitful life.

A founding piece of the new nature is honesty. The Christian is to walk in honesty, "putting away falsehood, let all of us speak the truth" (v. 25). The author describes and models the sort of truth-speaking appropriate to Christian life. The author speaks the truth and does not cover it over. This is seen when, immediately after exhorting to speak the truth, the author takes up the problem of anger. It would be easy enough to deny the existence of anger or to dismiss it, as is so common today, as a "secondary" emotion. Instead the author says, "Be angry" (v. 26). The honesty of this statement is refreshing in a time like ours. We would like to cover over anger, to avoid it, to deny its existence. But this text indicates that anger exists; there is no denying it. To walk the Christian walk, to live the life to which one has been called, does not mean all causes of anger will disappear. Nor does it mean sweetness and kindness precluding anger. To the contrary, the Christian walk described here will from time to time necessitate being angry—so Ephesians advises, "Be angry."

There is room for anger in the Christian community, but there is not room for unceasing anger. Recognizing the reality of anger, the author admonishes to "not let the sun go down on your anger" (v. 26). The community can tolerate anger, but it cannot long hold together if the anger is not confronted and worked out. The Christian walk does not end in strife, but rather the resolution of strife, the overcoming of enmity.

There is in popular culture a warped sense of Christian life as somehow being exempt from troubles and enveloped in a sort of "super" kindness. This portion of Ephesians does relate an admonition to kindness to being a Christian. To "be imitators of God" (5:1), one puts aside "bitterness and wrath and anger and wrangling and slander" (4:31). But these are admonitions placed in the context of an honest assessment of the way things are. Admonitions to kindness and urgings of forgiveness do not obliterate the reality of enmity and strife. Instead, it is precisely in the face of enmity and strife that kindness and forgiveness are called for.

To walk the Christian walk, to live in the sort of community Ephesians describes, where "we are members one of another" (v. 25), means confronting anger head on and facing difficulties without denying their existence. But more than this, it means working to resolve the troubles that confront us in the light of Christ's love. That is, the Christian walk is a "walk in love" (5:2). This is no syrupy or silly love, but a mature love that knows both the need for forgiveness and its joys.

The Christian walk being described in these verses is the walk of the baptized. The source for all such walking, all such loving, all such resolution of conflict is in the Holy Spirit (v. 30). The Holy Spirit has marked the Christian with the seal of redemption and provides the means of responding to the call to the Christian walk.

GOSPEL: JOHN 6:35-51

The story of manna in the wilderness is again referred to in this lection (v. 49). It is only a brief reference, but an instructive one. Jesus says, "Your ancestors ate the manna in the wilderness, and they died." Jesus' interpretation of the manna is a radical one. Normally the manna story is interpreted as the miraculous giving of life when death from starvation threatened. But in the emphasis Jesus places on the story, what is significant is that those who once ate manna are now dead. Potent as manna was in fending off death in the wilderness, it was a temporary victory over death's claim on the living. Sooner or later everyone must die, even those who have eaten manna.

In contrast to the transitory victory over death that is achieved by eating manna, Jesus makes the bold claim that he is the bread of life (v. 48), the living bread (v. 51), and those who eat this bread will not die (v. 50), but will live forever. The manna feeding was done once; the feeding of which Jesus speaks is once and for all.

At one level, of course, it is not true that one does not die—even Jesus dies. But this lection speaks on more than one level. In verse 36 Jesus identifies the failings of those who have followed him: they have seen and yet not believed. That is, they have only seen at one level and not yet seen at the level of which Jesus speaks. It is the will of the one who sent him, he goes on to say, that seeing be united with believing, and with believing comes eternal life (v. 40).

Again, in verse 42, those around Jesus only see on one level. Here Jesus is identified as the son of Joseph, and it is concluded that he cannot also be the bread of life that comes down from heaven. The point, however, is that it is precisely as son of Joseph that Jesus is also bread of life. There is more than one level operative here. Things are not just as they are; they are also as they will be through the work of the one who sent Jesus.

It is important to note what the work of God is in this lection. Unlike God's work in earlier verses, the principle work in these verses is teaching. " 'And they shall be taught by God.' Everyone who has heard and learned from the Father comes to me" (v. 45). In the earlier portion it was the ones who had been fed who did not see and believe. In verses 41-50 it is the Jews who do not see and believe. They had been taught, but had not learned. What they had learned, again, was only at one level.

The foundation for a true hope that reality is more than what appears to be depends on the teaching of God. Verse 45 contains a reference to what is written and what is "learned from the Father." Not that teaching alone gives hope. Teaching without concrete action, without bread in the present, is deceitful teaching and engenders false hope. Remember, however, that this talk of bread follows the concrete feeding of five thousand. When there is real feeding, tangible signs of hope, then there is need for teaching. What teaching enables is the vision to see reality at more than one level. In this sixth chapter of John, first there is feeding, then there is teaching, engendering a true hope.

This lection in the series of Johannine texts from the sixth chapter is located just prior to the most explicit language of the eucharistic liturgy. Undoubtedly the Eucharist as a practice is important to the Fourth Gospel writer, but it is never a eucharistic practice separated from actually feeding the hungry and teaching. Feeding the hungry is followed by teaching, which opens the way to seeing more than what at first appears before one's eyes. Only then is there bread to eat and wine to drink, body to partake and blood to drink.

The dreadful crisis we face in our time, not unlike the crisis in the time of the Fourth Gospel, is that we only see things as they are and have little inkling of what, in God's grace, they will be. We look at a troubled teenager and see only juvenile delinquency, not a child of God hungering for love. We look at deteriorating urban neighborhoods and see only poverty run amuck, not fragile communities thirsting for justice. Unless we see and believe, unless we imagine more than what we see, then what reality appears to be, is all that reality is, and will doubtless get worse. The teaching burden of the church may just be to renew our eyes to see and our imaginations to look afresh at the fuller reality. If we can believe that God promises more than what at first appears, then there is hope for even the deadliest of situations.

The Thirteenth Sunday after Pentecost

Lutheran	Roman Catholic	Episcopal	Common Lectionary
Prov. 9:1-6	Prov. 9:1-6	Prov. 9:1-6	2 Sam. 18:24-33
Eph. 5:15-20	Eph. 5:15-20	Eph. 5:15-20	Eph. 5:15-20
John 6:51-58	John 6:51-58	John 6:53-59	John 6:51-58

FIRST LESSON: PROVERBS 9:1-6

Given the placement of this text in the lectionary, it is easy to focus exclusively on the bread and wine. Indeed bread and wine figure prominently, but it is bread and wine served on a table in the house that Wisdom built. The significance of the table spread has everything to do with whose house in which it is served. This point is made especially clear by the parallel verses at the end of this chapter (vv. 13-18). In those verses wine and bread are served in the house of the foolish.

The allusion to the house that Wisdom built invites further scrutiny. The metaphor of house is a frequent one in the Hebrew Bible. Sometimes it is used to refer to the temple, at other times the monarchy, at still other times the family lines of the tribes of Israel. A common element in each of these uses is the structuring of a people or way of life over time or across generations. When this text says that "Wisdom has built her house," it means in part that Wisdom structures, or at the very least describes, a structure inherent in the way things are in the world. That is, Wisdom is an ordering of the universe, a way of holding the world together. This is seen again in the reference to the seven pillars (v. 1b) that hold the sky in place.

An invitation to a banquet set in the house Wisdom has built is an invitation to enter the balance of a particular world order. Clearly other candidates for the order of the world exist. The text describes one such alternate in verses 13-18. But for those who want to live (v. 6), for those who want understanding, the house of Wisdom is the only way.

In contemporary terms, the claims of Wisdom are not dissimilar to those who hope for an ecologically sensitive theology. That the physical and social world is structured and balanced in an intricate web of interrelationships is a conclusion difficult to deny. That attending to the structure of these interrelationships is both prudent and necessary for survival is patently true. Despite these truths, however, exactly how one finds the appropriate balance, or engages in the right social behavior for the desired end results is not so easily discerned. The more one knows about the delicate balances in the physical and social world, the more one grows suspicious of zealous efforts to right obvious wrongs. Often, well-intentioned efforts at solving the world's woes exacerbate the problems at hand. Minority hiring may result in tokenism; urban renewal may "gentrify" the poor out of housing; protection of wolves in a habitat without natural predators may threaten other species. This is not to discourage movements toward responsible and conscientious social behavior, surely such behavior is sorely needed. It is only a caution for the "simple" (v. 4) who might believe Wisdom is easily discerned and prudent courses are clearly marked. It is the same caution found in this chapter of Proverbs: "The fear of the LORD is the beginning of wisdom" (v. 10). Here is the counsel of humility. The word *fear* could also be translated "to hold in awe." The one who holds God in awe will not presume to know too much. Instead, those who fear the Lord know full well that there is no human way to fully grasp the structure of the universe.

Without such fear or awe, efforts to turn the order of things to our own advantage can proceed to disastrous consequence. Undoubtedly there are vast and glorious things to learn and marvelous and beneficial discoveries to be made. In all of these learnings and discoveries, wise is the one who is awed not by the human ability to discover, but by the remarkable power and craft of the Creator.

ALTERNATIVE FIRST LESSON: 2 SAMUEL 18:24-33

In the most powerful terms, this story describes David's reaction to the news of Absalom's death. He was moved, he wept, he wailed the grieving parent's wail: "O my son Absalom, my son, my son Absalom! Would I had died instead of you, O Absalom, my son, my son!" The son David grieves had turned against him. He had chosen to overthrow his father's kingdom and ultimately to kill his father. David knew that his son would die, but he could not face his son's dying. In a vain effort he instructed his armies to go gently with Absalom, but he knew it was not possible. David could not face the dying of his son. When the messenger comes he has no choice but to face his death; and it is his death he grieves.

In remarkable ways this story of David's grief over Absalom parallels the story of David's grief over the unnamed child recounted in 2 Samuel 12 (see The Eleventh Sunday after Pentecost). In that story David grieved the dying of the child, but did not grieve the child's death. Each story describes one half of the grief over death. On the one hand there is the grief over dying, a grief suffered even by the one who dies. On the other hand there is the grief over death, a grief suffered only by those who survive the one who dies. With the unnamed child, David only suffers one form of grief. With Absalom, David only suffers the other. The speed with which David recovers from his grief over the dying of his child stands in contrast to his inability to stop grieving over the death of Absalom. It is only after he is chided by Joab that David puts an end to his public grieving. The story hints that the private grieving will never end.

The full agony of death is not in dying itself. When the nameless child died, David stopped grieving. To only suffer the process of dying is to suffer the easiest portion of death. The hardest part of death is not the dying, but the living after the loved one dies. When this child Absalom died, David suffered potently. Why should Israel care about David's reaction to the death of his children? It is not altogether clear why the narrator is so interested in David's grief. Perhaps it is because a nation's people need to know if kings and others capable of committing a nation to war can suffer the full power of another's death. Perhaps it is because this king who has been anointed by God ought somehow to reflect the character of God, who in Jesus, Christians confess, knows both the agony of dying and the suffering of death.

Preaching on this text might be helped by locating a contemporary example of suffering both the dying of a loved one and the death of a loved one. The dual anguish is seen nowhere more poignantly in our time than with the families of AIDS patients. There are those families, who like David, are unable to withstand the dying and try to exempt themselves from the process of dying, but endlessly suffer the agony of the death of the loved one. And there are those families who enter both the suffering of the dying and the suffering of the death. The stigma of AIDS has also brought with it the deadliness of social isolation. All of these aspects of dying can broaden and deepen preaching on this text.

SECOND LESSON: EPHESIANS 5:15-20

Again the author of Ephesians acknowledges that there are choices to be made in the present. As the author observes, "the days are evil" (v. 16). In the face of such evil times, the Christian is to make careful and wise choices. The author exhorts one to walk as the wise do, "making the most of the time" (v. 16). The way to walk wisely and make the most of the time is to avoid making the wrong choices. The wrong choice described in this text is the choice of "drunkenness" leading to "debauchery" (v. 18). The choice to walk wisely is also to make a wise choice, and that is to choose thanksgiving to God.

According to this portion of Ephesians the most indispensable activity in an evil time is thanksgiving. To sing praises to the Lord is the most appropriate use of time. For those Christians of an activist bent, such counsel must surely seem ill-advised. Surely in an evil time, a time that might be like our own, the most prudent course is to take up the cause of justice and work diligently against all that is evil. For many concerned Christians today, Christians who perceive this to be an evil time when justice seems seldom to be found, making the most of the time must surely mean providing for those in need and transforming the systems of oppression and evil. The counsel to avoid drunkenness and "always and for everything giving thanks" must seem the height of absurdity, irrelevance, and prudishness.

It may of course be correct that the counsel of Ephesians is overly prudish, and somewhat irrelevant. There is much to suggest that this portion of Ephesians, taken as a whole, represents an overly moralistic approach, and for our time an especially conservative moralism at that. Nevertheless, the counsel to choose thanksgiving (*eucharisteō*) over drunkenness merits some attention.

When the choice is presented this way, as one between giving thanks or drunkenness, the deck is stacked. Only the most embittered or foolish person would choose drunkenness over giving thanks. But it is a sort of deck-stacking that places the focus on what we might today call a spiritual discipline. The result of drunkenness, as translated in the Revised Standard Version, is "debauchery." Although this is not a common English word, it is a good translation of the Greek *asōtia*, and literally means to be seduced away from one's work. To choose drunkenness leads to a dissipation of attention to one's work; it leads away from doing the will of the Lord (v. 17). To give thanks involves continually honoring the Lord's will and therefore placing it at the center of one's work. Such a spiritual discipline does not mean abandoning the very much needed work of caring for those in need and transforming systems of oppression; it does mean continually remembering why one is engaged in such activity.

Working for justice and caring for those in need is done, not because it is the socially acceptable thing to do, but because it is the will of God. It is very appropriate work in an evil time. It is work that Christians are called to take up in their Christian walk, because the Christian walk is finally walking in the paths opened by the will of God.

GOSPEL: JOHN 6:51-59

In these few verses the Fourth Gospel presents its version of the eucharistic words of institution. Although isolated elements of this discourse will be familiar to those accustomed to the church's communion liturgy, as a whole this version of the words of institution appears somewhat crude, even cannibalistic. The language is more jolting because, unlike the Synoptic Gospels, John does not retell the events of the Last Supper in the upper room. When in the other Gospels the account of the final meal is told, speech of eating and drinking the body and blood of Jesus is more readily seen as figurative language. When the words of institution are abstracted from the narrative of the table fellowship the result is a more graphic, even literal, description of eucharistic eating and drinking. Such is the case in John's Gospel. The link between bread and wine as emblems of Jesus' body and blood is weakened, because the only explicit talk of eucharistic eating and drinking is of flesh as "food indeed" and blood as "drink indeed."

It is important to examine more closely the purpose of John's writing. Whereas the Synoptic Gospels have a great stake in preserving, even constituting, the ritualistic practice of the early church, these practices are already established by the time John addresses the issue. That is, for John the issue is not establishing a eucharistic ritual, but interpreting an already practiced one. Most important for John is what is at stake in partaking of the Eucharist, namely, partaking in Jesus' future.

For John eucharistic practice is not optional in the community, but essential. Unless they eat of the living bread (v. 51) they may have life, but like all those who have gone before they will die and not rise (v. 58). Those who eat of the living bread, those who partake of Jesus (v. 56), will also partake of his relationship to the Father (v. 57), his resurrection (v. 54), and his future of eternal life (v. 54). These claims point to John's overriding concern about the Eucharist, namely that the community's life should conform to the life and death of Jesus and consequently share in his future. The future of those who do not partake of the bread, that is, the ones who are outside the Christian community, is marked by death's victory. Only those who eat of this bread, who share in Christ's future, have eternal life.

The community John addresses, like communities the preacher of this text will address, is already familiar with a eucharistic practice. Bread is eaten and wine is drunk as means of partaking in the life and death of Jesus. The temptation in our communities is that the bread and wine become commonplace. The shock, scandal, effrontery of this eating and drinking readily disappears into the regularity and familiarity of the ritual.

John is aware of the temptation of the commonplace; he is aware that seeing a sign can devolve into not seeing that which is signified by the sign ("Very truly, I tell you, you are looking for me, not because you saw signs, but because you ate your fill of the loaves," v. 26). It is for this reason that he collapses the distinction between the bread that is a sign for the flesh of Jesus and the flesh of Jesus itself, the very flesh that dies on a cross. By collapsing this distinction, John makes it clear that this bread is not just bread, it is instead "bread from heaven," "living bread." Through the bread that we eat, we abide not merely in a community that ritually eats bread and drinks wine, but a community whose life is wholly determined by the living and dying of Jesus, and so determined, shares his future of eternal life.

Exactly what it means for any particular community to be determined by the living and dying of Jesus and sharing in his future of eternal life will vary by circumstance and context. For a community facing overwhelming poverty, it will likely mean a hopeful horizon to human history in which the injustice of hunger and the anguish of premature dying is overcome. For a community of relative affluence, it will likely mean a judgment on present orderings of common life and renewed imagination for just living. For a community, impoverished or affluent, to whom dying is imminent, abiding in this way with Jesus will likely mean recognizing the stark and undeniable reality of death while finding assurance in the promise that the one who "eats this bread will live forever" (v. 58).

The Fourteenth Sunday after Pentecost

Lutheran	Roman Catholic	Episcopal	Common Lectionary
Josh. 24:1-2a, 14-18	Josh. 24:1-2a, 15-17, 18b	Josh. 24:1-2a, 14-25	2 Sam. 23:1-7
Eph. 5:21-31	Eph. 5:21-32	Eph. 5:21-33	Eph. 5:21-33
John 6:60-69	John 6:60-69	John 6:60-69	John 6:55-69

FIRST LESSON: JOSHUA 24:1-2a, 14-25

Joshua 24 is an account of the covenant renewal ceremony for Israel. Although ostensibly dated at the time of Joshua, the text clearly has many other settings in which it has been used and shaped. Israel's continual renewal of the covenant will regularly recall this story and its parallel stories in Deuteronomy.

It is possible, of course, to pick up the interpretation of this rich text at any number of points. An especially suggestive one, however, is the familiar phrase, "but as for me and my household, we will serve the LORD" (v. 15). Focusing interpretation on this phrase unfolds the conditional character of the relationship undergirding Israel's covenant renewal ceremony, a ceremony outlined in this text.

The conjunctive *but* returns the reader to a point immediately prior to the pledge to serve the Lord, when the option to do otherwise is set forth. Serving the Lord is not an accomplished fact, it is not a given; it is a choice. Contrary to a notion that there are no other gods to serve, this text makes the clear claim that the people might choose to serve other gods. The aim of this text is not to assert the truth of monotheism over the falsity of polytheism. Polytheism is an accepted fact; the choice is between the other gods and the God who "brought us and our ancestors up from . . . the house of slavery" (v. 17).

The choice to serve the Lord or not to serve is conditioned even further by the phrase "as for me and my house." In contrast to a response typical of American individualism, the commitment to serve the Lord is not solely an individual one. The speaker does not say simply "I will serve the Lord." Rather, it is both the individual and the individual's community (me and my house). The one who serves is not isolated from a community who serves. For this portion of Joshua, serving the Lord is not an individual action, but a communal one.

Recital of the Lord's deeds (vv. 16-18) reveals a significant element of serving the Lord communally. What the Lord has done was not done to this individual or that one, at some points not even to this generation; nevertheless, the speaker refers to what the Lord has done for "us." This is especially important when one considers the long dry spells there are in Israel's history. Forty years in the wilderness meant a full generation wandering without a home. The house that chooses the Lord endures as a community over time even when suffering afflicts individuals in the household. Serving communally therefore correlates to having been served as a community, even a community that has endured over time.

A final element should be noted. The ability to choose available to the people is likewise available to God. God has chosen to do "good" to the people (v. 20), but God could also choose to consume them and do them harm. There is much at stake in the relationship established in the covenant. Covenanting is not a one-way street. It involves not only God's choice, but ours. That a fruitful and faithful relationship results is truly a gift—a gracious gift—and not a given to be taken for granted.

ALTERNATIVE FIRST LESSON: 2 SAMUEL 23:1-7

When compared to the rich narratives concerning David, this lyrical affirmation of the Davidic monarchy is sterile and cool. Here David is an unconflicted ruler of the people, serving God in all faithfulness. The everlasting covenant made between God and David is described with its resultant benefits. David is richly blessed and his monarchy is secured.

It is especially suggestive to read this description of an unconditional covenant between God and David over against the covenant with Moses. The Mosaic covenant is not unconditional. It is conditioned on the choosing of God and people to serve each other. Both parties are free to choose otherwise. Undoubtedly there are consequences to such choosing, but choices are available. The Davidic covenant, "For he has made with me an everlasting covenant, ordered in all things and secure" (23:5), operates under an understanding that God has unconditionally covenanted to love this people and secure David's monarchy.

Since the lectionary has taken the reader of this text through the stories of David's infidelity, ruthlessness, and self-centeredness, this hymn praising the monarchy does not ring true. Only the most cautious affirmation of the Davidic monarchy is called for. For this reason it is especially important to note that the praise in this hymn is not finally sung to David, but to God. It is God who has established the covenant. It is God who freely chooses to covenant with David and upbuild his throne. It is God who rules justly and God who will consume all pretenders to the throne of God.

The significance of the opening of this lection, in which what follows is attributed to David's last words, is not in its direct connection with David, but in its connection with what will follow in David's place. Israel sings this song and remembers these words, not because of David, but because it establishes the relationship between the people and God. The rulers who are to follow in David's way, the ones who will sit on the Davidic throne, are not to do as David did, but as David was called by God to be. The ruler of Israel is to "rule over people justly" (v. 3). The song of praise to the monarchy does not describe what is, but prescribes what is to be if the ruler is faithful.

SECOND LESSON: EPHESIANS 5:21-33

No portion of Ephesians, and not many sections of the Bible have received more comment in recent years than this one. In an era such as ours, when the roles and relationships of women and men are so rapidly and drastically changing, this text understandably has received a great deal of attention. For some it represents divine sanction for what is termed "traditional" family life. For others it represents evidence of religious culpability for a sexist society. Some commentators have tried to show how egalitarian the author of Ephesians is—to the point of stretching an interpretation beyond reasonableness. Some have argued the outright rejection of this text and the purging of its influence. In the face of such division, how is this text to be preached, if at all?

There can be little doubt that an expectation of wives being submissive to their husbands finds support and justification in this text. Despite the most heroic efforts to interpret away this implication, it remains. Like it or not, the text argues for a social ordering that places women in a position subordinate to men.

One fruit of interpretative efforts to soften the blow of this text is a consensus that the treatment of women it urges is more egalitarian than was the prevailing custom. Many scholars have argued that the author of Ephesians has attempted to offer a Christianization of a customary "household code." Although this is heartening news, a relatively good social ordering hardly comforts the preacher who in good faith cannot promote or affirm such a social ordering. Relatively good can fall far short of good.

One way to preach this text without promoting its social ordering is to preach what the text does, not only what the text says. The text tries to Christianize a custom. It takes what in practice and in potentiality is a misogynistic custom and attempts to give it a Christian interpretation in which dehumanizing aspects are reduced. As a strategy for Christian social ethics, this is an appropriate model. Christians are called upon to live in the world, in cultures with existing customs. The call is not always to overthrow existing custom, but at times to interpretatively transform these customs. That is, at times Christians are called to find ways to redescribe and reinterpret what is done in a culture. Such a Christianizing of custom may make it possible for Christians to live authentic Christian lives in the world.

Of course, the greatest danger is that such an approach to living in a culture will dilute or distort Christian faith. That is, instead of Christianizing custom, it is possible to customize Christianity so drastically that it no longer can claim allegiance to the risen Christ. Rationalization can be substituted for transformation. The key to interpretation can be located in social conformity, rather than in living out Christian faith.

In an ironic way this is what our culture has done historically with this text from Ephesians. The original attempt to Christianize a local custom has become a theological and ecclesiastical customization of Christianity. The author's reinterpretation of custom in light of Christianity has became a reinterpretation of Christianity in light of custom. The treatment of women in the history of Western Christian culture has far too often been one of forced subordination justified theologically by this text. By misusing this text it has been possible to "baptize" abusive customs that have contributed to the dehumanization and oppression of women. The author of Ephesians took the prevailing practice and tried to transform it. The church has far too often taken what is there and tried to justify it with this passage from Ephesians.

Preaching this text will be difficult, because it will have to try to reverse a long standing history of misuse and abuse of both the text and the ones hurt by its misinterpretation. It may be that a faithful way to preach this text is to recognize that some customs are to be transformed and reinterpreted, which is what the author of Ephesians has done, and some customs are not to be tolerated and must be overthrown. Perhaps after thousands of years of misogyny, it is time to overthrow a custom as abusive as "the husband is the head of the wife."

GOSPEL: JOHN 6:60-69

The clinching line in this passage comes from the mouths of the disciples: "This teaching is difficult; who can accept it?" (v. 60). It is refreshing to find the Bible saying outright the very thing that sincerely religious folks so often feel. Much of what is said in the Fourth Gospel is hard to listen to. For that matter, much of the whole Bible is filled with hard sayings. But of all the places to say it, of all the places to finally come out and say how hard it is to listen to what Jesus says, why is it said here? After all, is it really that scandalous that Jesus speaks about eating his body and drinking his blood? Aren't there many things more scandalous than this?

Indeed, there are many more scandalous things. Jesus turns to the disciples and points to the most scandalous of all: "Does this offend (Greek: *skandalizō*) you? Then what if you were to see the Son of Man ascending where he was before?" (vv. 61-62). The reference to ascending is not a final ascension, but a reference to the cross. The real scandal, the toughest hard saying, the thing most difficult to listen to, is not talk of eating a body and drinking blood, but of breaking a body and spilling blood.

Throughout this sixth chapter, the focus has been on failure to see beyond the most obvious: on the mountainside with the five thousand, seeing beyond the limited resources to God's abundance; in the feeding itself, seeing beyond the food that perishes to the food that abides, beyond the work of human agents to the work of God. Again in this passage the focus is on seeing beyond the obvious. Looking beyond the eucharistic language of body and blood's obvious scandal to Jesus' broken body leads to the full scandal of belief. To believe Jesus is to have at the center of one's life the frightening realization that it is only the "spirit that gives life" (v. 63). All attempts to hold onto life, to create life, to possess life, are doomed to disaster, even as the bodily life of Jesus is doomed to disastrous demise. "The flesh is useless" (v. 63); it is not possible to hold onto the bodily, fleshly life, it will not endure. But to believe Jesus is also to know that the sum of life, the substance and majesty of life, is not restricted to bodily life, but to the enlivening power of spirit.

Although it is the clear statement of this text that the flesh is of no avail, it is extremely important that this statement remain in the full context of the chapter. Despite the ultimate futility of the flesh—after all, even the ones fed by manna will die—there is still an unavoidable need for actual feeding. Recall that the opening of the sixth chapter describes the recognition on Jesus' part that the crowd needed to be fed. It would be a mistake to think that the ultimate inadequacy of the flesh means that the concrete needs of everyday life are insignificant. On the contrary, there are great needs regularly addressed by Jesus.

The scandal, the truly hard saying is that we are unable to secure the feeding we need solely by our own devices. It will take much more to feed us than our own efforts. Looking at our own efforts will be like looking to the few fish and loaves available at the beginning of this chapter. They are not enough without the active care of God. For those among us, and this surely will mean a great many of us in affluent First World settings, who still hold on to some notion that we are capable of providing our own daily bread, the futility of the flesh is a hard saying that needs to be spoken again. By the same token, even the most self-assured person stumbles and falls freshly into the vulnerability from which the realization comes that our lives are but gifts given from the hand of God.

The last thing to note in this lection is the confession of Simon Peter. Many were so scandalized by the claims of Jesus that they "turned back and no longer went about with him" (v. 66). Jesus then turns to the disciples and asks if they too want to leave. Simon Peter answers that there is no where else to go, because Jesus is the only way to eternal life. A chapter filled with complaints about the inability to see finally has a success. It is a hard saying to have to receive life as a gift and not be able to secure it for oneself. But as Simon Peter rightly confesses, there is no other way. Life is either given as a gift, or there is no life. Without the gift of life, there is only the continual holding back of death, fighting it off here and then there, to eventually and inevitably fail.

The Fifteenth Sunday after Pentecost

Lutheran	Roman Catholic	Episcopal	Common Lectionary
Deut. 4:1-2, 6-8	Deut. 4:1-2, 6-8	Deut. 4:1-9	1 Kings 2:1-4, 10-12
Eph. 6:10-20	James 1:17-18, 21b-22, 27	Eph. 6:10-20	Eph. 6:10-20
Mark 7:1-8, 14-15, 21-23	Mark 7:1-8, 14-15, 21-23	Mark 7:1-8, 14-15, 21-23	Mark 7:1-8, 14-15, 21-23

FIRST LESSON: DEUTERONOMY 4:1-9

Occasionally it is useful to consult a different biblical translation to catch a nuance missed. Such is the case in this Deuteronomy text. Two fairly uncommon English words appear in the King James Version that are worth reconsidering: *cleave* and *nigh*.

At verse 4 the King James Version reads, "ye that did cleave unto the Lord." The word *cleave* has almost completely disappeared from English usage. It is a very odd word, because depending on its usage it can either mean "adhere to" *or* "separate, tear apart." In one usage, *cleave* means to "split apart" as in what a cleaver does. In the other usage, the one intended by this translation, it means "to hold to, to cling to, to stick to something." The meaning that suggests sticking to or clinging carries with it the notion that such a clinging is over against an underlying cleavage. To cleave to the Lord then, is to hold onto the Lord despite the deep and obvious separation between the Lord and the people.

Another seldom used English word found in the King James Version is *nigh*. *Nigh* refers to something that is near by or close at hand. It is this latter usage that captures part of the nuance of this text. The ambiguity of the phrase "the kingdom of God is at hand," is similar to the ambiguity in the statement "God is nigh." It means that God is very close, but its meaning implies at the same time a distance. "God is nigh" means that "God is not yet fully present." To be nigh is not to be here, but still at some distance, no matter how small.

Nuances among English translations do not necessarily represent parallel nuances in the Hebrew text. Despite this caution, the pericope does share in the thematic tone of proximity to God despite undeniable separation. The call to heed the commandments, the statutes, and ordinances is issued as a means for this and subsequent generations to stay near the Lord. The possibility of straying from this God is made especially clear by the prohibition of adding to the commandments (v. 2). To add to the commandments is to swerve off the narrow course that maintains proximity to God.

Such proximity assures life (v. 4); swerving from the course threatens destruction (v. 3).

Living closely with God, living obedient and faithful lives, is truly called for. The fruit of such living is nearness to God, but not full presence. The separation between God and human beings persists.

ALTERNATIVE FIRST LESSON: 1 KINGS 2:1-4, 10-12

As part of the succession narrative of the Davidic monarchy, this brief lection stands as an interlude in a story of palace intrigue. The power plays, political maneuvering, threats, and deceptions that mark the ascension to the throne of Solomon are interrupted briefly for this last speech of David. This insertion bears the mark of the Deuteronomist, later generations pointing back to the early warnings that finally have led to the demise of the nation. One could imagine these generations lamenting, "If only Solomon had done as his father said." If only Solomon and the kings who followed would have "walked in the ways of the Lord."

In many ways this interlude is about the transfer of power in the state. There are two sorts of power in the state: power assumed and power given. The verses that precede this pericope speak of the transfer of occupants of the throne, the assumption of power. This lection, however, speaks of the transfer of traditions, the gift of power from the hand of another. The traditions of Moses and David are to be transferred to the new occupant of the Davidic throne. The problem with Solomon is that he is more interested in thrones than traditions.

It is not really enough to simply have power given by the tradition. It also requires laying claim to the power given, assuming power. By the same token it will not do to simply assume power; it must also be given. As the law of Moses was passed to David, so he here passes it on to Solomon. To Solomon it sounds like the ramblings of a senile old man. To the generations who suffer the scourge of Solomon's cruel rule, it sounds like the counsel of the wise.

At the points of transition in our lives we are apt to look for those things we can grasp as signs of stability, those things that will help us rest secure. The most stable point, if we are to listen to this text, is in the traditions that are passed from one generation to another.

SECOND LESSON: EPHESIANS 6:10-20

The use of military metaphors in this concluding section of Ephesians overshadows a more subtle shift in metaphors. Up until this point, walking has been a frequent metaphor in Ephesians, but here the metaphor shifts from walking to standing. In verse 11 the reason for putting on the "whole armor of God" is to be able "to stand" against the wiles of the devil. In verse 13, again the armor is mentioned and again it is called upon to be able to "withstand" (v. 13a), "to stand" (v. 13b) and again to "stand therefore, and fasten the belt of truth around your waist" (v. 14a).

Throughout, the letter to Ephesians has exhorted its readers to a way of life, a Christian walk, that is distinct from other walks or ways of life. The author has tried to describe aspects of that life and to draw a contrast between the Christian life and other lives. The frequent use of the metaphor "walk" has emphasized aspects of movement and journey. The church is called to a journey with Christ, to live a holy and righteous life in relationship with God. The metaphor "walk" connotes a Christian life that is not stagnant or sedentary, but on the move, alive, and lively. The author has also conveyed that it will not be an easy journey; there will be threats and fears and conflicts along the way. Some of those conflicts will be from without and some from within the church.

In this section, as throughout Ephesians, there is no direct reference to the source of conflicts. That is, no particular historic persons or groups are named. It would be fair to say that for Ephesians the sources of conflict are not located in a person or a party, but in a power or a principality (v. 12). To overcome a conflict that is unable to be fixed in a particular person or party requires taking a stand. The military metaphor would work differently if it were possible to identify the "bad guys," but as Ephesians indicates, they may not be easily associated with personages of "flesh and blood." Instead it may be necessary to discern the "spiritual hosts of wickedness" wherever they light. To do this will require taking a firm stand in faith, appropriating truth and becoming clear on the gospel.

The most adequate parallel in our day may have to do with doctrinal clarity. The church in our day often wavers on what it believes about matters of faith. Occasionally the church locates an enemy in some political movement—be it a "red menace" or "raving capitalist." Ephesians warns that it may not be so easy to locate a threat to faith so clearly. It may be necessary to see the presence of a threat in the presence of a friend as well as in the presence of a stranger. To overcome the conflicts that face us, we need to understand that they are ambiguous and that our resources are to be found in prayer, the gifts of the Spirit, and the proclamation of the gospel.

GOSPEL: MARK 7:1-8, 14-15, 21-23

The most apparent meaning of this lection could be summarized as a criticism of surface things and a call for deep things. A summary such as this links Mark's text to a prophetic tradition critical of cultic practice in the absence of justice practice. What really matters, what is most urgent, is not that this rule or law is followed obsessively, but that justice and righteousness are practiced. In the words of this pericope, the "commandment of God" takes precedence over human traditions (v. 8).

It is difficult to dispute this interpretation, as it is a fairly obvious and straightforward meaning. It rests on a long tradition of prophetic preaching. It addresses a recurrent problem in human endeavors, the problem of forgetting what one is doing by getting lost in the way one does it. However, beyond the obvious meaning of this text, Mark is doing something else that needs attention. Unfortunately, the versification suggested by the lectionary overlooks the movement of the text and it is in the movement that another aspect of interpretation becomes possible.

There are three sections in Mark 7:1-23, each delimited by the audience Jesus addresses. In the first section (vv. 1-13), Jesus speaks to the Pharisees. In the second section, Jesus speaks to the "people," presumably those who have gathered around him (vv. 14-16). In the third and final section (vv. 17-23), he addresses the disciples. In each section Jesus repeats the same essential lesson.

In the first address Jesus defends the practice of his disciples (eating with unwashed hands) by turning the offense against the Pharisees: "You abandon the commandment of God and hold to human tradition" (v. 8). Jesus intensifies his criticism of the Pharisees, concluding with the charge that they have made "void the word of God" (v. 13).

In the second address Jesus speaks to the crowd, and the tone is quite different from that used with the Pharisees. His tone is more didactic or hortatory, as he gives the crowd a simple summary of the teaching he began with the Pharisees. To paraphrase, one might say, "externals are not important, it's what is inside that counts."

In the third address Jesus speaks to the disciples and again gives the lesson on externals versus internals. In this third address one begins to grasp that the central lesson is not simply a repetition of the prophetic teaching concerning justice and righteousness, but a plea for deepened understanding.

In this portion, as in so many other portions of Mark's Gospel, Mark again portrays the disciples as not understanding. In perhaps the strongest language of the Gospel, Mark describes Jesus' frustration with the disciples because they do not "understand either." In an ironic twist, Jesus then proceeds to tell them again. The irony is this: If it were completely true that only what was inside a person mattered, there would be no reason for

Jesus (or Mark after Jesus, for that matter) to explain again the lesson. Explaining is outside a person; it is an external exercise. But it is not the case that one can never learn. Mark writes in the hope of convincing the readers that the gospel is true and conversion is called for (Mark 1:15). The point is not simply that one should not fuss over externals, but that the important things, the good news itself, is to be so internalized, so thoroughly understood, that it will affect all of one's external actions. For Mark, conversion is just such an internalization of the gospel.

This point is evident in the movement of the text. In the first interchange, Jesus defends the disciples against the Pharisees' criticism. By the last interchange, Jesus too criticizes the disciples. Jesus' criticism, however, is not that they have eaten with hands defiled, but that they have failed to "understand." The disciples have appropriately been free from fretting over externals, but they have not fittingly fretted over internals. The call to the hearers of Mark's Gospel is to be free from fretting over the externals, while paying close attention to the internals. Once the gospel is internalized, the external behavior will follow in response.

The Sixteenth Sunday after Pentecost

Lutheran	Roman Catholic	Episcopal	Common Lectionary
Isa. 35:4-7a	Isa. 35:4-7a	Isa. 35:4-7a	Prov. 2:1-8
James 1:17-22, 26-27	James 2:1-5	James 1:17-27	James 1:17-27
Mark 7:31-37	Mark 7:31-37	Mark 7:31-37	Mark 7:31-37

FIRST LESSON: ISAIAH 35:4-7a

The rich and glorious poetry of Isaiah of Jerusalem is here in full bloom. The images of restoration and reversal, of healing and hope, are so strong one is easily caught up in their power. The opening of blind eyes, the unstopping of deaf ears, and the singing of a mute tongue are all justly to be celebrated. Add to this the breaking forth of water in the desert and the resultant renewal of forsaken land. Isaiah, the poet of the peaceable kingdom (11:6-9), again ignites the imagination for a new day, a hopeful day.

The Sixteenth Sunday after Pentecost

The hopeful day Isaiah describes is clearly not the present day, but a future one. Although the vision of hope is so powerful that it is difficult to imagine a time or circumstance in which it did not exist, the prophet can easily imagine a time without hope. It is the genius of this prophet to speak a word of hope when there are so few signs of it. Isaiah is not reading the signs in the political arena and forecasting that all is going to turn out for the best. Such a prediction would amount to optimism and not hope. The difference is this: optimism is a positive expectation of the future based on evidence in the present; hope is a positive expectation of the future based on God's faithfulness.

Contemporary North American congregations, at least those middle class in circumstances, are far too often willing to accept optimism instead of hope. Some scholars have even termed ours an officially optimistic society. We often want to believe that things are getting better everyday in a natural process of improvement. Such is not the situation out of which Isaiah speaks. Although this is one of the most beautiful texts in Isaiah, and if taken by itself it would indicate that Isaiah knows only the vision of peace and wholeness to come, Isaiah knows more. The prophet speaks hope over against surrounding troubles. The situation at hand does not leave ground for optimism, but requires vision beyond the present. God is bringing the hope that is to come.

In some ways this text will not find an appropriate hearing in comfortable settings. It is easy to misread the powerful words of promise as a *description* of what God is doing already for the successful and not as a *prescription* of what God will do for those who live in wilderness and desert. Isaiah's powerful language will likely find a proper home in the desert and wilderness, in those places where life is hardly worth living. It is only in such places where this language of promised triumph over adversaries is able to avoid a dangerous triumphalism. God is not blessing the status quo and providing Isaiah with the words for sanctioning things as they are. Instead, Isaiah's words are of God's dissatisfaction with the way things are and God's longing for the redemption of the people.

There is a triumph promised, a beautiful triumph in which all that is amiss will be set right. Isaiah speaks forcefully of this promise, and the church is right to share in Isaiah's promise-making speech. But it must remember that promisemaking depends on God's faithful *promisekeeping*, not our successful working.

ALTERNATIVE FIRST LESSON: PROVERBS 2:1-8

The student of wisdom is charged to "treasure up my commandments" (v. 1), that is, the student is given the task of memorizing what is taught.

The text itself is filled with mnemonic devices. Like the little rhyme that helps one memorize the length of the months, this lection is structured to help the student remember what is taught. "Treasure up," the wisdom teacher says, remember, memorize, store what is learned and don't forget it.

Fearful that rote memorization had taken the place of real learning, for a time many modern educators abandoned the art of memorizing. Memorizing, however, is what is called for by this proverb. Make what you are taught so much a part of you that you can call upon it without even thinking. Make it so much a part of the way you walk or talk or do anything in your life that it will be automatically retrievable. Clearly memorizing by itself is not enough, but it still goes far in the journey toward understanding.

So much of life falls into the abyss of forgetfulness. Recovery of some aspect of memorizing could serve us well. The only real danger of memorization is that one loses the desire to learn more. It is this desire that the wisdom teacher promotes by calling for the student to "cry out for insight." Picture that child in the classroom, so eager to speak she can hardly stay still in her seat, waving her hand, eagerly waiting to be called upon by the teacher. "Cry out for insight."

SECOND LESSON: JAMES 1:17-27

It is often difficult to find strong connections between portions of the book of James. Frequently the verses stand independently as individual teachings. To a certain extent, that is the case with this portion. There are many quotable quotes in these verses, which could be abstracted from their context. They include phrases like: "Every generous act of giving, with every perfect gift, is from above" (v. 17), or "be doers of the word and not merely hearers" (v. 22). Nevertheless, an overarching issue arises in these verses, namely, the relation between hearing and doing.

The first mention of hearing comes in verse 19, when the counsel is given to be "quick to hear." This counsel forms the foundation of the repeated tension between hearing and doing. When the author makes the point that people are "blessed in their doing" (v. 25), it is a blessing that has grown out of hearing. To be "quick to hear" in itself is not enough; being slow to forget and taking action on what is heard is also required.

In contemporary terms one might say that to be "quick to hear" is to heed the early warning signs. The point the author of James makes is that by itself being "quick to hear" is not enough. It is as if a person discovered a small cancerous growth in the early stages, but then neglected to take any action to excise the growth or retard its progression. All the advantage of an early warning is lost if no action is taken to end the problem.

The metaphor, "be quick to hear," indicates the need to carefully attend to what is going on, to discern from the full mix of events and voices that surround us the appropriate situation to which a response is called. This leads to the second point in these verses in which hearing is mentioned (v. 22). To be quick to hear is to pick out what is important to hear. Those hearers who deceive themselves hear only what they want to hear and do not listen carefully enough to what is going on.

Persons who wear hearing aids often report that it is difficult to sort out which sounds are important and which are not. Apparently hearing aids often amplify everything and do not discriminate between sounds. The person who wears a hearing aid must learn anew how to discern which sounds are worthy of response and which need to be ignored. All listening is an exercise of selectivity. When James speaks of hearers who deceive themselves, he is speaking of those whose selective listening has excluded what should not have been heard. They are like those who have failed to heed early warning signs of cancer, even when they know full well how dangerous it is.

How does one exercise an appropriate selective listening? It is not completely clear in this portion of James, but it might just be that one does so by referring to the "implanted word." The implanted word, or the human conscience, will lead one to attend to the important aspects of a situation.

The third place where hearing is mentioned refers to hearers who forget. To hear is not to have what is heard go in one ear and out the other, but to be so shaped by the hearing that a response comes forth. In all of this portion of James, doing provides the full complement for hearing. Hearing that does not follow with doing is no hearing at all. To hear the word of God is to discern its consequences for this situation and this time.

These practical words of James provide an important challenge for the church today. It is fitting for us to attend with great care to the call to listen and carefully respond to the word of God and the urgent needs of our times.

GOSPEL: MARK 7:31-37

Mark is either a poor geographer or is up to something else in presenting the travel itinerary at the beginning of this pericope. Trying to retrace on a map the movements of this journey from "Tyre . . . by way of Sidon towards the Sea of Galilee, in the region of the Decapolis" will lead in the most circuitous, if not impossible meandering. It is difficult to know what Mark is up to in this strange geographic sequence—perhaps nothing more than an attempt to emphasize the extent of Jesus' mission to the Gentiles.

After this confusing introduction there lie two events: the healing of the deaf/mute and the repudiation of the charge to silence. Both events share a common theme, namely, the speech that arises out of an encounter with Jesus. Despite this shared theme they represent two distinct reactions to Jesus. The first reaction to an encounter with Jesus, the reaction of the man healed, is to speak clearly. The second reaction, that of the witnesses to the healing, is to speak zealously.

The action of the text is as follows: A man deaf from birth with an impediment in his speech is brought to Jesus to be healed; Jesus heals him, but only after an intricate ritual and a final pronouncement that Mark is careful to give in Aramaic; the man healed speaks clearly; Jesus charges the crowd not to talk about this event; and immediately the crowd does the opposite—zealously proclaiming what Jesus had just forbid.

There are three speakers in this pericope: Jesus, the man who is healed, and the crowd. Each represents three distinct types of speech: freeing speech, the speech of freedom, and free speech. The first type of speech belongs to Jesus. Although Jesus utilizes a variety of ritualistic activities, it is only after he utters the word *Ephphatha*, only after he speaks, that the healing occurs. The speech of Jesus sets the man's tongue free. In fact, the description of the man's healing is literally that "the chains of his tongue were broken." This speech of Jesus is *freeing speech*. It is powerful speech, so powerful that it can even be heard by one who does not normally hear.

The second type of speech is that of the man healed. Once healed, his tongue is liberated and he speaks clearly, freely. One whose tongue had been bound is set free. His speech is the *speech of freedom,* the newfound clarity of one able to finally speak. It is the expressive speech that gives voice to the joy of freedom from oppression. Other examples of this sort of speech of freedom can be found in Miriam's song in Exod. 15:21.

The third type of speech is that of the crowd. They could speak all along. They are charged to silence by Jesus, but they are not silent. Their speech is *free speech.* It is important to note that the free speech of the crowd is neither freeing speech (that is, it does not effect freedom), nor is it the speech of freedom (that is, the clear expressive speech of the newly liberated).

For those of us who so dearly value free speech, it is instructive to note the differences in these types of speaking. Speech that liberates, that has the power to set free, is the most profound and necessary speech for living.

It is for the protection of this kind of speech that the United States Constitution guaranteed free speech. Without this freeing speech there is little future for our common life. Speech that sets free can be as politically charged as the words of the Emancipation Proclamation, or the whispered, intimate "I love you." Freeing speech breaks downs the walls of isolation and oppression.

Having the ability to speak freely is not the same thing as engaging in freeing speech or the speech of freedom. Just because one can talk doesn't mean it is always appropriate to talk. The real value of what we call free speech is not found in the freedom to say whatever one wants no matter whom it hurts or who has asked us to do otherwise. The real value is in the power of speech to liberate, to create freedom, or to express freedom. Speech that expresses freedom, the speech of freedom, is the second kind of speech described in this text. It is the spontaneous speech of the newly liberated. When freedom comes there is no stopping the joyous outburst of speech. One thinks of the strains of the Gloria sung after the words of assurance in the liturgy of the church, or the spontaneous outburst of celebrative joy when a patient learns the tumor removed was benign, free from the threat of cancer. Perhaps the most common speech of freedom is praise. It verbally acknowledges the gift of freedom.

The speech appropriate to the gospel is the freeing speech of Jesus or the speech of freedom of the man healed; it is not the free speech of the crowds. When the crowds had seen what Jesus had done, they were amazed and went about zealously saying what they had seen. Jesus, however, had explicitly charged them to silence. What was the harm in their zeal? Why are they not free to speak as they wish?

Although free speech formally means that one can say whatever one pleases, such is not the real freedom of speech. The real freedom of speech is not simply saying what one pleases, it is speaking for the sake of and in the name of freedom. When Jesus charges the crowds to silence, they do not heed his request. They do not speak because they have been freed, but because they have been amazed. Their speech is little more than the gossip of those who gawkingly attend to the affairs of others. There is no doubt that they have the right to speak freely, even over the objection of Jesus. Having a right, however, does not constitute freedom; freedom is truly gained when a right is exercised responsibly. The church is called to take up freeing speech and to share in the speech of freedom; only then will there be meaningful free speech.

The Seventeenth Sunday after Pentecost

Lutheran	Roman Catholic	Episcopal	Common Lectionary
Isa. 50:4-10	Isa. 50:5-9a	Isa. 50:4-9	Prov. 22:1-2, 8-9
James 2:1-5, 8-10, 14-18	James 2:14-18	James 2:1-5, 8-10, 14-18	James 2:1-5, 8-10, 14-18
Mark 8:27-35	Mark 8:27-35	Mark 8:27-38	Mark 8:27-38

FIRST LESSON: ISAIAH 50:4-9

The portion of Isaiah in which this lection falls is commonly called Deutero-Isaiah. The prophecy found in Deutero-Isaiah articulates a word of hope to an exiled people. Beginning with the call to comfort in chap. 40, and throughout the fifteen chapters of this portion of Isaiah, the prophet speaks of an approaching newness. A thematic focus for the entire prophecy can be found in Isa. 42:9: "See, the former things have come to pass, and new things I now declare; before they spring forth, I tell you of them." The newness that is coming is not yet present, but it can surely be counted on. Throughout the prophecy, Isaiah asserts and attests to the power of God. God's power to create is touted (see 43:1, 44:2), vastness is proclaimed (see 40:12, 21ff.), and incommensurability is exclaimed (49:15, 55:9). It is the one who is so powerful, so vast and incommensurate, who will do the new thing of which the prophet speaks. The newness promised by a God of such characteristics (see the contrast between this God and all others in 44:9-20) will surely be worth waiting for.

The theme of newness forms an implicit context for this lection as well. In the third of four servant songs, the servant speaks of the help of God (vv. 7, 9), while lamenting the abuse of adversaries (v. 6). The help of God is not yet present, but it will arrive; when it does, the servant will be vindicated and the adversaries will be consumed. It is the new thing God is doing that will vindicate the servant and punish the adversaries, but more importantly it is trust in the new thing of God that makes it possible for the servant to endure.

In verse 7 the servant says "I have set my face like flint." Flint is emblematic of the hard posture of one who is determined to endure. In stark contrast the adversaries of the servant are compared to garments (v. 9). Like garments they will eventually wear out and be consumed by a moth. The adversaries will not be able to hold on; they lack the flintlike determination of the servant. The servant, whose help is the Lord God, will not be worn out, but will endure and eventually prevail.

Even knowing that the servant will prevail does not make the waiting easy. Waiting on the day when the servant will prevail is hard. It is because it is so hard that the servant is not only described as one who has been given the "tongue of a teacher" (v. 4), but also is daily given ears to hear God. To endure the trials that come to the servant requires faith in God to do a new thing and daily speaking and hearing of the promises of God.

This lection, while directly speaking *of* the servant, speaks *to* the exiled people of Judah. Through the servant song the prophet is commending to the exiled people a way of relating to God and a means of dealing with adversaries. The servant is vigilant for God, speaks for God, listens to God. So too, the exiled people are to listen, speak, and be vigilant. The servant withstands the abuse of adversaries and anticipates their demise. Again, indirectly the people are commended to do the same.

Identifying adversaries of the contemporary congregation will undoubtedly result in a cluster quite distinct from those of either the servant or the exiled people. Nevertheless, there are contemporary adversaries. How are we to endure in the face of those things that threaten our lives? The lection gives clues. Through listening to the promise of God and awaiting the new thing God will do, it is possible to hold on to an undying hope.

ALTERNATIVE FIRST LESSON: PROVERBS 22:1-2, 8-9

The four verses of the lection are related to each other only in that they are each wisdom sayings and each, to a greater or lesser extent, address the relations between wealth and poverty. It would be a mistake to try to make them fit together organically, much as it would be a mistake to attempt to find an organic connection between "an apple a day keeps the doctor away" and "a penny saved is a penny earned." Only after each proverb is examined on its own terms is it advisable to attempt an overarching interpretation.

The proverb found in Prov. 22:1 does not condemn wealth. It advocates a priority of reputation over wealth. Consistent with wisdom teaching, wealth can be a fruit of faithful living or it can be a fruit of greed, cunning, and deceit. It is this ambiguity of wealth that lies behind the saying. Wealth without a good reputation is not to be chosen. The one who has wealth and a bad reputation will have gained wealth unwisely. Holding together a good reputation and wealth is the most preferable of options. This is so not because they are both admirable things, but because wealth gained at the cost of a good reputation is ill-gotten gain. If a choice is to be made between wealth and a good reputation, the clear choice is a good reputation.

The proverb in verse 2 is a descriptive saying. It gives warrant to a belief in a divine design for the distribution of wealth. Some are wealthy, some are poor, all are made by God, says the proverb. In the proverb no attempt is made to probe the mind of God. That is, there is no attempt to discern why such an order exists. There is only the frank description of economic circumstance and the assertion of a ground of commonality. It is the ground of commonality that is worthy of special note. By definition poverty brings with it great sources of anguish and pain, especially inadequate resources for daily life. In addition, however, there is often exclusion from the sources of power in common life. Implied in this proverb is the claim that the wealthy and the poor, although divided by the resources at their disposal, are not to be divided by their access to social, political, and religious power. The proverb suggests that economic distinctions need not necessarily be religous, political, class, or social distinctions. Wealth and poverty cast solely in economic terms is a radically different understanding of poverty from that most prevalent in our day.

The proverb in verse 8 uses a metaphor of planting and harvest to express the relation between injustice and evil. The injustice that is sown will come back as evil. Complicity with injustice in the short run may not be costly. In the long run, according to this proverb, the costs of injustice will be great.

While the first half of the proverb in verse 9 ascribes blessing to the generous, the second half defines generosity. To be generous is to share one's own bread with the poor. Extending care to the poor is a source of blessing.

Taken together, these proverbs form a web of relations between the poor and the rich. The plight of the poor and the plight of the rich are inextricably bound together. It goes without saying that the plight of the poor is bound to that of the rich. What is not as obvious and requires saying is that the plight of the rich is bound to that of the poor. The wisdom teachers know that without generosity, justice, and honesty, wealth will have been gained at the expense of another. Sooner or later it will come time to for the rich to pay.

These proverbs make points that are worth making again. In our current economic climate, with the gap between the rich and the poor widening, it is important to say aloud that both are bound together. If the wisdom teachers are correct, the poor and the rich, created by God, share a future together or they have no future at all.

SECOND LESSON: JAMES 2:1-5, 8-10, 14-18

It is of great importance that the tremendously powerful and imminently preachable phrase "faith by itself, if it has no works, is dead," comes as it does in a discourse on the poor. It is of great importance, because faith without works is a luxury only those who are not poor can afford. When faith tries to live without works, it is not just faith itself that dies, it is literally the poor who die. The consequences of a faith separated from works is the perpetuation of deadly systems that make it possible for some to go without "daily food" (v. 15). When faith, if it is truly possible to call such a thing faith, does not find its complement in acts of love and compassion, justice and care, feeding and clothing, then the consequence is death.

Latin American theologians, who have in recent years made many in the church freshly aware of the poor, frequently define poverty as dying before one's time. The works called for by faith are works that ensure none of God's children die before their time. Faith finds its life and brings life when it is manifested in life-giving works.

There is an important distinction to get clear in this text concerning who may and who may not show partiality. The text exhorts the person of faith to show no partiality. Its example is the giving of a special place to a rich one over a poor one. The person of faith, who could easily be tempted to show partiality to a rich one, is charged to show no partiality at all. This point is important. At least until verse 9, there is an implication that if one doesn't show partiality to the rich one, then it is good to show partiality to the poor. The admonition, however is to show *no* partiality. The poor and the rich are to be treated without partiality by the person of faith.

At the same time, the text gives clear indication that God does show partiality. God is partial to the poor: "God has chosen those who are poor in the world to be rich in faith and heirs of the kingdom" (v. 5). This special choosing by God is clearly a showing of partiality on the part of God. What are we to make of this? God unabashedly shows partiality; the person of faith is charged not to show partiality. On the one hand, one can affirm the saying of Isaiah that God's ways are not our ways and God's thoughts are not our thoughts. There is good reason to again make this affirmation. On the other hand, it is also important to see a connection between what God does and what the person of faith does. God gives life through God's partiality. God's partiality to the poor means that the creation will not be finished until the poor are made rich in faith and have become heirs to the kingdom. Our impartiality preserves the life God gives. It does not seek to place one over another, but places both rich and poor on equal footing in our common life. God's partiality and our impartiality share a common objective—the fostering and preservation of life.

GOSPEL: MARK 8:27-38

The episodes in this text mark a turning point in the Gospel. In these brief verses is contained the naming of Jesus as Messiah, the first passion prediction, and the last teaching before the transfiguration. The center of this set of episodes is the saying on suffering.

The confession of Peter that Jesus is the Christ is immediately followed with a charge to tell no one. The charge to secrecy is common in the Gospel of Mark, and the educated reader is not surprised to see it here. What is surprising is that in the next episode, in which Jesus predicts his suffering, rejection, and death, the text states that "he said all this quite openly" (v. 32). Peter's naming of Jesus as the Christ, the Messiah, the one to come, is set in secrecy. Jesus' prediction of suffering, rejection, and death are said openly. Suffering gets publicity; messiahship gets hidden.

The charge to secrecy in the Gospel of Mark characteristically follows a healing or miraculous working by Jesus. In this case it follows not a healing, but the naming of Jesus as Messiah. The charge to silence, although frequently disobeyed, serves as a way of indicating that the miracle is not the way to fully identify Jesus. Even the title Messiah, which Mark wants to be associated with Jesus, is not fully correct. It needs further interpretation, which we find in verses 31-33. The identity of Jesus as Messiah is completed only by connecting it to the suffering of Jesus. To be the Messiah does not just include miraculous healings or events; it has at its core suffering. The ones who want to have a Messiah without suffering have not understood Jesus and do not yet know what it means that he is the Messiah.

Ironically it is Peter, having just named Jesus as the Messiah, who now misunderstands completely. Peter has been a witness to much of what Jesus has done and makes the correct confession, but fails to grasp its significance. Peter does not understand that suffering is integral to the messiahship of Jesus. That Jesus must suffer distresses Peter; he will not have it. Surely Jesus has used the wrong word. Not suffer, he couldn't mean suffer. But that is the word Jesus uses; he says suffer. It is the right word. And what is more, it is the word of God. It is God's word—suffer. "Get behind me, Satan! For you are not on the side of God" (v. 33). To be on the side of God is to suffer. Jesus said it plainly and openly. If the miraculous life-giving power of Jesus is to be observed and embraced, if Jesus is to be publicly proclaimed as the Messiah, it will have to be done with cognizance of suffering. The secret can be broken as long as everyone is clear about the suffering.

The final episode of this lection addresses the necessity of suffering for all of the followers of Jesus. To follow Jesus is to come to terms with suffering, to take it up. To take up one's cross is to take up suffering and join with the Messiah whose messiahship is marked by suffering.

By and large, we try to deny suffering. Peter tried to deny it—"Oh no, there will be no suffering here!" A lot of us are like Peter; we want to deny that there is suffering. But there it is—it is everywhere. There is no denying it. Children get cancer; marriages fail; jobs are lost; people are hungry and homeless, or just plain lonely. There is no escaping suffering. To be on the side of God is to stop denying that there is suffering.

When the church of Jesus Christ fails to take the suffering of the world seriously, it loses all connection to the crucified and risen Messiah. The church often does just this. In recent years, the mainline church has become inordinately concerned with its own institutional life. With decreasing membership and declining revenues, the church has tried to find ways to increase its numbers and enhance its financial resources. Undoubtedly these are important matters for the vitality of the church but they can be seductive matters. Vitality in the church is not necessarily something to be sought, or sought primarily. Faithfulness in the church *is* to be sought. Faithfulness in the church will require regularly taking up the cross. It will mean placing unrelenting concern for suffering at the center of the life of the church.

An unrelenting concern for suffering is not an embrace of suffering as a treasured value. It is instead a frank acknowledgement that suffering is everywhere and a recognition that the ministry and mission of Jesus is to a suffering world. The church that fails to share this mission will no longer be faithful and perhaps will eventually no longer be vital.

The Eighteenth Sunday after Pentecost

Lutheran	Roman Catholic	Episcopal	Common Lectionary
Jer. 11:18-20	Wisd. 2:12, 17-20	Wisd. 1:16—2:1, 12-22	Job 28:20-28
James 3:16—4:6	James 3:16—4:3	James 3:16—4:6	James 3:13-18
Mark 9:30-37	Mark 9:30-37	Mark 9:30-37	Mark 9:30-37

FIRST LESSON: JEREMIAH 11:18-20

These few verses form the first of a series of personal laments in the book of Jeremiah. Complaints spoken to God thus concern the enmity against the prophet by his adversaries. It is unclear from these verses who the adversaries are, but it is clear that they want to do away with Jeremiah.

These and other complaints by Jeremiah in the prophetic book teach the cost of prophecy to the prophet himself. From this text it begins to be clear that Jeremiah is vulnerable to threats and assaults from those to whom he speaks. His prophecy is not welcomed or received as a "friendly reminder," but constitutes a genuine challenge to its hearers. Inclusion of these complaints in the book of Jeremiah give more than an insight into the life of the prophet; they also give a sense of what the prophet provoked. Jeremiah's speech so upset the powers that be that they were provoked to do away with him.

The three threats or schemes that Jeremiah recounts (v. 19b) indicate that the forces against him would not be satisfied with simply silencing him. That would not be enough; it would be necessary to completely obliterate what he said. Jeremiah's prophecy, which was bold enough to say that things in Judah were not as pleasant as they seemed, could not be tolerated by the holders of political, social, and religious power. Jeremiah had been so bold as to challenge the official optimism of the day. He had said that things were not as they were being described. In 6:13-15 for instance, he says: "From the least to the greatest of them, everyone is greedy for unjust gain; and from prophet to priest, everyone deals falsely. They have treated the wound of my people carelessly, saying 'Peace, peace,' when there is no peace. They acted shamefully, they committed abomination; yet they were not ashamed; they did not know how to blush." Jeremiah had displayed the audacity to call the leaders liars and thiefs. He had pierced the official propaganda that had been promoting a perception of peace when there was no genuine peace. He would not let them get away with the charade that things were "hunky-dory" when they were a mess.

For the crime of speaking the truth his adversaries want to do away with him. The text describes destroying not just the fruit of the tree, but the tree itself; cutting off from the land of the living; and doing away with the memory of Jeremiah. Among the three forms of eradication planned for this trouble-maker, the third one is most telling. To remove Jeremiah from the memory of the people is among the most severe forms of eradication. In Israel, remembering and being remembered are critical aspects of living. In Isaiah the exiled people thought that God had forgotten them, to which they are answered with the hopeful words, "I will not forget you" (Isa. 49:1-15). In Genesis, God remembers Noah (Gen. 8:1), Abraham (Gen. 9:16), and Rachel (Gen. 30:22); and with each remembering, life is given. To be remembered is to be preserved or restored in the community; it is constitutive of life. When schemes are being made to wipe Jeremiah out of the memory of the people, drastic measures are being taken. If the memory of the people can be controlled, then life itself can be controlled.

Jeremiah complains about these schemes and prays God's judgment be executed against those who scheme against him. It may be that Jeremiah is simply trying to save his own skin. Or it may be that Jeremiah, and those who have preserved this text, are trying to save the people from any who would try to eradicate their memory. If one can be made to forget, then it is possible to believe that the way things are is how things are supposed to be. If one can forget, if the memories of hopes and dreams can be shunted, then the status quo can be preserved. The greatest danger to freedom and justice is amnesia. Without memories of promises made and kept, there remain no grounds for hoping. Jeremiah's adversaries know how dangerous memories are; they know that if the people remember, they will not be happy with the way things are. Knowing this, they want to wipe out Jeremiah, because he keeps bringing up memories of God's faithfulness and the people's faithlessness. If only they can do away with the memory of these things and the memory of Jeremiah, they could have their way.

In our relatively comfortable lives it is easy to be lulled into forgetfulness. It is easy to forget disturbing memories. It is easy to believe that we were always meant to have it so good or earned what we have. It easy to forget what we received as a gift and all who do not have it so good. It is Jeremiah's prayer that God will not let the memories fade. Jeremiah laments, complains, prays that God will judge righteously and stop those who will wipe out the people's memory. It is fitting in our time to join Jeremiah in this prayer, praying for the judgment of God, so that the memories that are the basis of hope will be kept alive.

ALTERNATIVE FIRST LESSON: JOB 28:20-28

This portion of the book of Job follows the arguments of Job's three friends. Although it is placed in this location, it could easily have been placed elsewhere. The text makes no direct reference to Job, his circumstances, or his friends. Instead it is a poem on wisdom that describes the hidden nature of things.

The order and design of the universe is too vast and complex for creatures to comprehend. In the language of the text: "It is hidden from the eyes of all living, and concealed from the birds of the air" (v. 21). The creature cannot comprehend the creation, only the Creator can. Again in the words of the text: "God understands the way to it, and he knows its place" (v. 23).

This text focuses on the limits of the creature's knowledge and the fullness of the Creator's knowledge. Only the Creator knows why and how things are.

In some ways it is unfortunate that this text is placed where it is. The probing of Job into the meaning of his suffering, his persistent challenge of God, his defense against his friends, can too easily be dismissed if this text is misread. This text is not yet a resolution to Job's dilemma. To be sure, it accurately forecasts the conclusion that Job will reach, but it is too early in Job's quest for him to find such resolve in resignation. The text should be read as a background piece in the story. As an overture gives a foretaste of the theme to be developed in a musical drama, so too this text gives a foretaste of the resolution to be reached. The text is background in the story of Job's suffering; it cannot become foreground until Job persists in his questioning and challenging of God.

The sort of arrogance Job's friends display when they come with ready answers to Job's suffering is a constant human temptation. A zeal to resolve dilemmas, to place suffering in a manageable context, fails to grasp the power of suffering experienced and not simply explained. If the lection for this day is used as a means of explaining suffering, of setting it in the grand and inexplicable design of the Creator, then it is reduced to the sort of arrogance of Job's friends. Instead this text is a theme song, repeatedly sung, but not readily grasped in its full significance. It is background music—elevator music if you will—that is, until one experiences firsthand the devastation of suffering. Only then can the words of the text have meaning beyond the obvious truism. When the questions suffering provokes have run their course, then the words of this text return: "Where is the place of understanding? It is hidden from the eyes of all living" (vv. 20-21).

In many ways the hymnody of the church is analogous to this text. Rarely are the hymns we sing explored for their significance. They are most often sung, year in and year out, and that is the way it ought to be. We do not need to understand their meaning immediately. Hymns that are apparent nonsense in one time may in some future time break open with new meaning. Although hymns are sung frequently, a hymn will often only have meaning on the particular day when what it says and what we need to hear are in coincidence. This text in Job does not yet speak to Job, but it is sung nonetheless.

SECOND LESSON: JAMES 3:13—4:6

This lection moves from the pursuit of wisdom and understanding to the giving of strong advice concerning moral life. Its range includes concern about truth, murder, adultery, and peace. The issues that lie behind these far-reaching concerns are not easily identified. Despite this difficulty, it is possible to locate a thematic focus in dominant metaphors the author uses.

The book of James liberally uses spatial metaphors. The faith one has *inside* is to find expression in works *outside*; wisdom and understanding are from *above*, evil and sin are from *below*. With more spatial metaphors this lection pursues an inquiry into the source of wisdom and the source of disputes. The epistle writer describes a wisdom that comes from above (v. 17). Such wisdom is to be contrasted to "earthly, unspiritual, devilish" (v. 15) wisdom. The writer queries further, "Those conflicts and disputes among you, where do they come from?" to which the answer is given, "From the cravings that are at war within you" (4:1). The line between good and evil, above and below, is clearly drawn. The source of good is from above, from God. The source of evil is from below, from within the one who is too earthly.

Spatial metaphors persist when the writer quotes Scripture, saying: "God yearns jealously for the spirit that he has made to dwell in us" (4:5). This quoted language is a key to interpreting these verses. The chasm between what is above and below is bridged by God's work to make the spirit "dwell in us." The movement from above to below is also a movement from God who is outside of us to the spirit who is inside us. This movement across spatial lines is the foundation for all of the virtues listed in James, which include: wisdom, understanding, mercy, good fruits, gentleness, purity, peace, righteousness. It is not enough, however, to simply follow the movement from God who is above to the spirit that is within. The full logic of this epistle requires the spirit that is within to make the movement into good works in the external world.

A final warning in this text has to do with "friendship with the world." Such friendship with the world, the epistle warns, is tantamount to enmity with God (v. 4). It would be a mistake to think that James is urging a rejection of concern for the world. Indeed, few portions of the New Testament have more persistent concern for the world. It is instead the case that James wants to be sure that the focus of concern for the world does not come from the world into the believer. Instead, it is concern implanted within the believer by God that makes it both possible and necessary to address the problems of the world. The believer does not take cues from the world for his or her concern; such would be "friendship" with the world.

For the contemporary church, this warning about friendship with the world is worthy of special note. The church is indeed to care for the world and the people of the world. However, often the church draws its agenda for "worldly" care from the world itself. The church may lose the uniqueness of its care for the world by assuming alternate modes of caring. For instance, concern about the psychological health of persons in the world is a legitimate concern for the church, but the church finally must discern its own definition of psychological health and not simply accept medical or therapeutic models. Likewise, the church is rightly concerned about the alignment of various political powers, but this concern is never just the same as that of any political party. To be faithful in its service and care in the world, the church must be led by fidelity to God.

GOSPEL: MARK 9:30-37

This text begins with the second prediction of the passion. It is in the context of this prediction that the rest of the text unfolds. Furthermore, it is the statement (in verse 32) that the disciples did not understand what he was saying that summarizes what is being said. Mark is making the point that the disciples do not and cannot understand what Jesus says about his suffering, death, and resurrection.

The disciples do not understand, because they cannot understand. Finally, it is impossible to understand what Jesus says about his suffering, until that suffering occurs. Suffering predicted is not the same as suffering witnessed. It will not be possible for the disciples to understand the teaching of Jesus concerning his suffering, or anything else for that matter, until they are witnesses to his passion.

The Eighteenth Sunday after Pentecost

Trying to teach the disciples about the suffering Jesus must endure is something like trying to teach an adolescent about the dangers of driving an automobile. One can tell horror stories of terrible automobile accidents. One can give endless recitations of fatality statistics. One can show pictures of mangled automobiles and injured passengers. All of these are of little or no use until the adolescent gains some sense of mortality, some hint of life's fragility. It may just be that until one looks into the jaws of death and pulls back with a gasp, all the teaching concerning driving safety falls on rocky ground.

For Mark, everything about Jesus must be interpreted through the lens of the cross. Without a grasp of the significance of the cross, everything Jesus says fails to get through to the disciples. The passion of Jesus undergirds the logic behind the teaching of Jesus. Without a grasp of this passion, the disciples are doomed to misunderstand his teaching. Although this is true of the disciples, Mark hopes it is not true of the reader of the Gospel. The reader, living on the "other side" of the passion, has available an opportunity to understand the teaching of Jesus afresh.

Following the statement that the disciples fail to understand what Jesus says concerning the passion, Mark alludes to a petty argument they have concerning who was the greatest among them. The argument is so childish as to be laughable. Mark's original audience, as well as the contemporary reader, easily recognizes the childishness of the disciple's argument. To debate the relative greatness of one over another in the face of the devastation Jesus has just predicted is akin to rearranging the deck furniture on the Titanic. It is simply nonsense to "fuss" over relative merit when the kingdom Jesus has come to usher in (Mark 1:15) is approaching.

Jesus gathers the disciples around and teaches them one more time in the paradoxical logic of the kingdom. The first will be the last. He reiterates the point by picking up a child, one incapable of greatness on the basis of merit. To welcome the child is to welcome both Jesus and the one who sent Jesus.

The logic the disciples fail to grasp reverses all worldly categories of power, prestige, and merit. The logic of the teaching of Jesus is in radical vulnerability. To be vulnerable, as a child is vulnerable, is to be open to the power of loving that is the central teaching of Jesus. Such loving, separated from the reality of suffering, however, is no loving at all. The love that Jesus embodies and that characterizes the kingdom of God unflinchingly delves into the depths of suffering. It is only in vulnerability that one grasps the power of such loving. This the disciples fail to understand and will not understand until after the crucifixion of Jesus.

The Nineteenth Sunday after Pentecost

Lutheran	Roman Catholic	Episcopal	Common Lectionary
Num. 11:4-6, 10-16, 24-29	Num. 11:25-29	Num. 11:4-6, 10-16, 24-29	Job 42:1-6
James 4:7-12	James 5:1-6	James 4:7-12	James 4:13-17, 5:7-11
Mark 9:38-50	Mark 9:38-50	Mark 9:38-50	Mark 9:38-50

FIRST LESSON: NUMBERS 11:4-6, 10-16, 24-29

The richly textured story that is excerpted in this lection should be read in its entirety. It weaves together several strands into an intricate narrative of origin in the life of Israel. If one attends carefully to the text, it is almost possible to hear the questions of subsequent generations for which this text gives answer. Behind the text are at least three questions: Why do we have a division of labor and leadership in our midst? Who are the legitimate leaders? How much can the community rightly expect from its leaders and from God?

The story begins with the complaint of the people of Israel concerning the paucity of their diet. The tradition of the people's complaint and God's gracious response is altered here, when God responds with rage and destruction. The people have asked too much; they are whining, and God will not tolerate it. The whining continues, however, and the brunt of it falls on Moses. Moses turns to God, and with a marvelous series of maternal images indicates that is was God who gave birth to these people, not he, and it is high time God take on some of the burden of leading them. Moses says, "I am not able to carry all this people alone, for they are too heavy for me" (v. 14). And so begins Israel's first bureaucracy, a form of labor and leadership division. Seventy elders are gathered and responsibility is shared. The story culminates with two episodes. In the first the people are given the meat for which they had been asking. Two young men, not elders, begin prophesying. The meat that is given makes the people sick. The new unauthorized prophets are given leeway.

This is a dense narrative with multiple themes and ample angles of focus for preaching. It is risky to reduce the text to a single theme or focus. Nevertheless, there is room for exploring the theme of legitimacy. What constitutes legitimate need and legitimate leadership? The text fractures sources of legitimation too easily obtained and suggests more subtle means of discernment.

As the people of Israel cry for food, they practice a behavior that previously assured them survival. When they were hungry before, they cried, God heard, and manna was provided. Now, again they cry, but this time they are first rebuked, then punished for crying. Lest the people believe that they were fed simply because they had cried out, the narrative suggests that feeding is in response to need, not want. Such a distinction between need and want is subtle.

The leadership of Moses was charismatic and authenticated by divine calling. The development of a council of elders, the seventy of which the text speaks, is not directly charismatic, but designated: "Gather for me seventy of the elders of Israel, whom *you know* to be the elders of the people and officers over them" (v. 16). The seventy are selected by Moses. They serve first by virtue of office and only derivatively by divine sanction. This is not to suggest that theirs is an illegitimate leadership. On the contrary, it is a legitimate leadership, authenticated by God's parcelling out a portion of the spirit placed on Moses. Despite the authenticity of this form of leadership, the narrative asserts the persistence, if not priority, of charismatic leadership. Lest the newly appointed leaders or the people of Israel begin to take the newly formed bureaucracy too seriously, the story is told of the two undesignated prophets whom even Moses recognizes.

Already in the wilderness the people of Israel are in need of means of ordering their life. They seek ways to establish practices and procedures for living. There is no thoroughgoing resistance to establishing practices, but there is ample caution about allowing the practices to run awry. As Israel learns, and every thriving community knows, it is at the subtle places where the practices and procedures fracture that faithful living occurs.

ALTERNATIVE FIRST LESSON: JOB 42:1-6

This lection is the concluding poetic section of the book of Job. It ends with Job repenting in "dust and ashes." Job, having been afflicted by God, having suffered at the hands of God, concludes by repentance. From what does Job repent? Were the accusing friends correct? Had Job done something which provoked God's wrath? No, the suffering Job experienced was too great to have a human antecedent. The source of his repentance must have been somewhere else.

A key to the interpretation of this text is in the contrast between the hearing and seeing. No new knowledge has come to Job, but new insight has come to him. Having heard from before that the ways of God are mysterious and beyond measure, he now understands it in ways previously unimaginable. Job pursued the most natural and persistent question for the one who suffers. He asked, Why? The one who suffers knows that no answer to this question will be able to exhaust the agony of the question. The question "why" is an endless question. Job did not come to the end of the question, he only came to a new understanding of the mystery of God, whose ways are inscrutable.

The book of Job is about theodicy. The word *theodicy* literally means to justify God. What Job saw was that it is not possible for a human being to justify God. It is the sin of seeking to justify God from which Job repents. Only God can justify God.

The prose conclusion following the poetic core of Job reverses Job's suffering, and restores him to his prior position. In many ways it is a distressing ending, because it is not much like the actual lives of those who suffer. Rarely does life provide such happy endings. This ending does, however, serve to sanction the questioning of Job. It would be wrong to take Job's repentance as an indication that the response of Job to the suffering he endured was inappropriate. On the contrary, his response is the only correct one, because it is the only honest one.

SECOND LESSON: JAMES 4:7-17

The book of James is filled with "good advice" for the person of faith. The maxims and aphorisms that constitute the book often do not tie together. Sequential placement of verses does not necessarily indicate thematic unity. Despite the absence of a verse-to-verse unity, there is a unifying thrust to the book. James is concerned with social justice. The human treatment of the people of the world, especially the poor, is of great concern.

The concern for social justice finds expression throughout the book. In the verses of this lection, the concern takes an almost existential form. The author asks, "What is your life? For you are a mist that appears for a little time and then vanishes" (v. 14). The brevity of one's life, the reality of finitude, radically relativizes designs for personal gain. Obedience is called for: "Instead you ought to say, 'If the Lord wishes, we will live and do this or that'" (v. 15). The text points to the folly of individual effort. No individual can know what tomorrow will bring. In the absence of clarity concerning the fates of the day, the person of faith follows the lead of God. The leading of God is found not in personal ambitions, but in the wisdom teachings, of which the epistle gives an ample dose.

There is an urgency to the preaching of this text in our time. Few organizations, secular or sacred, have escaped the triumph of "planning" as a mode of organizational life. Endless planning cycles are adopted. Five-year plans, three-year plans, short-term and long range plans, proliferate. There is no doubt that such planning serves a good and useful purpose, often adding intentionality to otherwise random activities. There is, however, a seductive temptation inherent in planning. Planning makes assumptions about its ability to predict the future. Planning assumes that the future can be controlled and managed. The Epistle of James doubts it. The future is more capricious than we care to admit. Our designs on the future can lead us into believing that we are the masters of our own fate. To such a belief the Epistle of James charges, "You boast in your arrogance" (v. 16). Planning is not an evil in itself. With proper humility, with openness to the leading of God, planning can help the one who knows "the right thing to do" (v. 17) to find a way to do it.

GOSPEL: MARK 9:38-50

This lection is made up of three independent literary units. The first, verses 38-41, is a story about an unknown exorcist and addresses the issue of boundaries in the community. The second, verses 42-47, is a string of comparative statements concerning the importance of unity of purpose. The third, verses 49-50, is an obscure saying concerning salt, with little relation to the whole.

The first of the three units begins with John, presumably one of the disciples, describing a recent encounter with someone who was casting out demons in the name of Jesus. John indicates that he and the others stopped this person because "he was not following us" (v. 38). Perhaps most significant is John's identification of "us." That there is some group capable of being identified as an "us" is what is really at stake in this story. Who can be included in an "us"? Who is to be excluded? John apparently has some criteria for exclusion, because he stopped the unknown exorcist. Jesus, by contrast, warns not to stop him, saying instead that any who accomplishes a "deed of power in my name" (v. 39) will sooner or later be a part of "us." The aphorism, "whoever is not against us is for us" (v. 40), radically extends the boundaries of the group and constitutes a broad "us."

Who can be a follower of Jesus? This is surely a lively question in the community Mark addresses. The telling of the story concerning the unauthorized exorcist is an attempt by Mark to respond to this question in his community. It is difficult to know with any certainty the form the issue of community boundaries took in the community Mark addresses. It would appear, however, that there was some attempt to test who was a "true" believer. Over against a testing for true belief, this text suggests that discerning who is genuinely against the community is the most important issue.

Undoubtedly boundaries are crucial for any community's life. The Christian church, in the first century or the twentieth, must be concerned with what constitutes genuine community identity and membership. In the light of this text, the establishment of boundaries is less to be determined from positive affirmations and more from negative threats. That is, those who threaten the community are rightly to be excluded. If it is not possible to discern a threat to the community, inclusion is to be assumed. The community of followers of Jesus is to include all, until some indication is given that they are "against us."

The second of the units in this lection is marked by a sequence of highly stylized repetitive phrases. The formula for the phrases is "if stumble . . . better to . . . than to." It is better to do away with whatever it is that causes one to stumble than to suffer the consequences of stumbling. What is stumbling? The Greek word for which stumble is the translation is *skandalizō*. It is appropriately translated "stumble," but it is also sometimes translated "take offense." The word, of course, is also the root for the English word "scandalize." To stumble is to be so scandalized that one is unable to attend to the matter at hand.

In the context of the prior unit's focus on inclusion and exclusion in the community, where inclusion is allowed to any who are not against "us," this reading of stumbling takes on a new meaning. Although the grounds for exclusion were narrowly focused on those that are "against us," what it means to be "against us" now includes whatever distracts from the central calling of the community. That is, to be scandalized, to stumble, is the ground for exclusion, or, even more powerfully, for excision. The text makes reference to "cutting off" the member who causes one to stumble.

The combination of these two texts creates a counterbalance between a broadly inclusive community and a strictly formed community with harsh means of exclusion. To be a part of the community that follows Jesus is first broadly defined as *not* being against Jesus. Then, however, what it means to be "against" Jesus is given specificity as anything that causes one to stumble, to be offended, to be distracted from the faith. To fall from faith is the worse fall of all. It leads to burning in the realm of hell.

It is extremely important to gain clarity about the notion of hell that is operative in this text. Dante's *Inferno* came long after the Gospel of Mark, yet contemporary readers of Mark are more familiar with Dante's vision of hell than with Mark's. Mark does not develop a doctrine of eternal damnation, with all the careful layers of burning and suffering. Instead, Mark borrows a ready-at-hand reference to a location outside of Jerusalem

The Nineteenth Sunday after Pentecost

where trash is burned. Hell is not the place where sinners burn for eternity down under the surface of the earth. It is, rather, a metaphor for a wasted existence. The cost of being "thrown into hell" is the cost of ultimate exclusion from the community. Freeing congregations from literalistic notions of hell and damnation should likewise free them for the powerful implications of the metaphoric use of hell. In the context of this text, whatever distracts one from the central calling of the community leads ultimately to exclusion from the community.

The final unit of this text is an obscure and confusing reference to salt. Clearly Mark has incorporated aspects of a saying from elsewhere into this text. Since the Gospel of Mark is liberally sprinkled with mnemonic devices—memory tricks—that help the hearer or reader to grasp what is being said, it is quite possible that this unit gets attached to the previous one because of its reference to fire. The device of repetition makes it easier to remember what is said, and sometimes, as in this text, it is nearly the only thread that holds the texts together. The only other aspect that ties this unit to the two previous ones is the phrase, "Salt is good, but if salt has lost its saltiness, how can you season it?" (v. 50). Without the essence of salt (namely, its saltiness), it is useless and ultimately disposable. The same is true of members of the community who have lost the essence of the community; they too are useless and ultimately to be disposed of.